HANOI

DANA FILEK-GIBSON

Contents

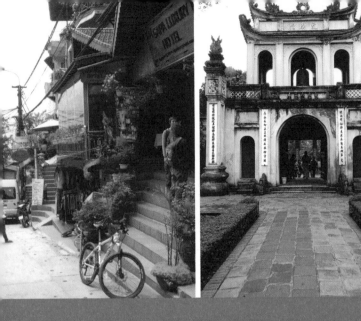

DISCOVER
Hanoi

I n a thousand-year-old city, you would expect some things to get lost in the mix, obscured by cramped shops and narrow houses or buried under the incessant blare of traffic. But along the busy streets of Hanoi, every era of the city's history shines— in its gracefully aging cathedral, sturdy Communist architecture, and the vibrant Old Quarter. Wander the bustling shopping streets of its older neighborhoods. Dive into history at the Temple of Literature. Visit the embalmed remains of Ho Chi Minh, Vietnam's most respected national hero. No matter what you do, there's no denying that the soul of Vietnam lies in Hanoi.

The capital is sleek and sophisticated. A well-established art scene and strong café culture permeate most of the city, along with a self-assuredness that comes from having survived a millennium of ups and downs. Flashy boutiques and shopping malls are beginning

Clockwise from top left: Sapa Luxury Hotel; the Temple of Literature; transporting goods via motor scooter; H'mong women in the Sapa market; a bowl of *bun bo*.

to make an appearance around town, a stark contrast to the narrow, teetering tube houses of the city's downtown districts.

Most travelers to Vietnam pass through the capital, not only for its sights, sounds, and savory cuisine, but also for its status as a hub, connecting popular destinations like Sapa with the rest of Vietnam.

Hanoi is a place to savor rather than sightsee. While its eclectic attractions make for a fascinating, patchwork history, the main draw of the capital is its infectious energy, which permeates every nook and cranny.

Clockwise from top left: H'mong children in Cat Cat Village; a mobile barber shop on a Hanoi street; goods for sale in the Sapa market.

Planning Your Trip

When to Go

The best months for exploring Vietnam are **September-October** or **April-June,** when you'll encounter warm temperatures and plenty of sunshine. **High season,** which tends to be chilly and misty, runs outside of both these times, with visitor numbers peaking **November-March.** Things get especially busy over Christmas before sliding into **Tet** (Vietnamese Lunar New Year) the following month. While this is a holiday of fascinating local traditions, it makes for a poor visit, as the entire country shuts down for weeks before and after. Those businesses that remain open often hike their prices to double or triple the usual amount, and transportation is unreliable. This time of year can also get bone chillingly cold up north, with fog often obstructing views. While fewer foreigners travel during the summer, sweltering **July** and **August** see droves of domestic holidaymakers.

Before You Go

Passports and Visas

Visitors are required to secure a **tourist visa** prior to arrival in Vietnam. This can be arranged through any Vietnamese embassy or consulate up to six months before your trip. In 2016, the Vietnamese government debuted a one-year, **multiple-entry tourist visa** for US passport holders. The visa costs USD$135-220 and allows American citizens to stay in the country for a period of up to three months at a time.

Additionally, US citizens can apply for one- and three-month visas with both single- and multiple-entry options. Depending upon both the nature of the visa and where you apply for it—whether through your local embassy or consulate, or via an online service—the short-term visas cost USD$75-180, while the year-long visa will set you back as much as USD$220.

Travelers entering Vietnam over land must visit an embassy or consulate to prepare their visa ahead of time. Air travelers have the additional option to apply for **pre-approval,** a significantly more cost-effective route, though this is only available to those arriving at one of Vietnam's three major airports: **Tan Son Nhat**

Tet decorations for sale

in Ho Chi Minh City; **Noi Bai** in Hanoi; or **Danang International Airport.** Although pre-approval is not encouraged by the Vietnamese government, it is a legitimate option, provided you arrange your documents through a reliable company. International air travelers must have a passport with at least six months' validity at time of travel.

Vaccinations

While there are **no required vaccinations** for Vietnam, the Centers for Disease Control recommend that travelers vaccinate against **Hepatitis A** and **typhoid** prior to visiting in order to prevent food-borne illness. Additional preventative measures, such as the **rabies vaccine,** are suggested for cyclists and those who may come into contact with animals. Vaccination against **Hepatitis B** and **Japanese encephalitis** are also recommended for some travelers, depending upon your destination.

Though **malaria** does exist in Vietnam, its prevalence is low. Most travelers opt to use insect repellent and cover up at dawn and dusk.

Transportation

Travelers to Hanoi will arrive at **Noi Bai International Airport** and set off from there. **Public transportation** is easily accessible, from planes and trains to buses and boats. For shorter journeys, hitting the road is the cheapest option; for long-distance trips, you're better off in the air or on the rails. **Budget airlines** like Jetstar and VietJet fly to a number of domestic destinations, while **overnight trains** run the spectrum from cheap hard-seat cars to air-conditioned sleeper berths.

What to Pack

Most Western amenities are available in Vietnam, though some are more affordable and accessible than others. **Sunscreen,** for instance, is available in many coastal destinations, though it can be tricky to find and is always more expensive. It's best to bring your own from home. Other items, like **contact lens solution** and **feminine products,** can be difficult to come by.

Vietnam tends to be **more formal** than the United States. In rural areas and outside of major hubs like Ho Chi Minh City and Hanoi, local women often dress more conservatively than their Western counterparts, opting for long pants and covered shoulders. Many Vietnamese women in the city have adopted a Western approach to fashion. You can get away with shorts, T-shirts, and tank tops in most tourist destinations. When visiting pagodas or sights of national importance, it's important for both men and women to opt for **conservative clothing,** wearing **long pants** and **covering shoulders,** as this is considered a sign of respect.

Hanoi can get deceptively cold in the winter. Though temperatures usually only drop into the mid-50s Fahrenheit at their lowest, coupled with the humidity and a lack of indoor heating, this means you should pack an extra layer or two, as well as waterproof outerwear.

The Best of Hanoi

Spend a weekend in the capital city, focusing on the hectic, narrow alleys of the Old Quarter.

Day 1

Touch down at Hanoi's **Noi Bai International Airport** and head toward the city. Dive right into the action with a cyclo ride around the **Old Quarter,** taking in its frenetic pace from the safety of your seat. Stroll around the placid **Hoan Kiem Lake** to see where locals hang out and catch a glimpse of **Turtle Tower** and the ornate **Ngoc Son Temple.** You can grab lunch in the Old Quarter or head to the clutch of cafés and restaurants around **St. Joseph's Cathedral** before charting a course south to **Hoa Lo Prison** and the **Vietnamese Women's Museum.**

Wind down the day on the streets of the chic **French Quarter,** either atop the **Press Club** terrace or at the roadside **Tadioto.** In the evening, grab dinner at **Ngon** before catching a **water puppet** or *ca tru* (ancient chamber music) show in the Old Quarter.

Day 2

Rise early for a morning bowl of pho, Hanoi's favorite breakfast food, before heading off to **Ba Dinh Square** to line up for a visit at **Ho Chi Minh Mausoleum.** Once you've paid your respects, swing by Uncle Ho's famed **stilt house** or head to the nearby **One Pillar Pagoda** for a different era of Hanoian history. From there, the **Military History Museum,** flanked by the **Flag Tower** and **Lenin Park,** is just a short walk away.

Turtle Tower on Hoan Kiem Lake

residents of a minority village in Sapa

In keeping with the Communist spirit, stop for coffee at **Cong Caphe** or head straight down to **KOTO** for lunch. Spend the afternoon getting to know Hanoi's **Temple of Literature** before wandering back toward the Old Quarter. Once traffic picks up and rush hour is in full swing, head for some *bia hoi* (freshly brewed light beer) and a night on the town.

Excursion: North to Mountainous Sapa

Head to Sapa, where you can opt to trek through Vietnam's **northern mountains**, visiting **remote villages.**

DAYS 3-4

Catch an overnight train from Hanoi and head to **Sapa.** You'll arrive in Lao Cai in the morning and take a quick minibus ride to the small mountain town. Take the rest of the morning to explore the town, passing by its **museum** and shopping along **Cau May** street. In the afternoon, head to **Cat Cat village** or hire a motorbike to visit the nearby **waterfalls** and **Tram Ton Pass.** You'll also want to arrange a **trek** for the following day, either through a local guide or one of the tour outfits in town.

Rise early and set off with your local guide to one of the nearby **minority villages** and get a more intimate look at the varied cultures of Vietnam. The trek takes a few hours, including lunch. In the afternoon, return to Sapa for a bit of R&R and any last-minute shopping before heading back to Hanoi via overnight train or bus.

Best Food

- **Xoi Yen:** A Hanoi institution, Xoi Yen slings bowls of savory sticky rice morning, noon, and night.

- *Bun cha:* The unsung hero of Hanoian street food, *bun cha* is an unbeatable combination of rice noodles, grilled pork, fresh greens, and pickled veggies.

- **Hanoi Social Club:** For an eclectic menu of both Vietnamese and Western contemporary cuisine, head to Hanoi's unofficial hipster hangout.

- *Chao suon:* A perfect breakfast or midday snack, this piping hot rice porridge topped with tasty fried dough and pork floss is doled out by no-nonsense women at the top of Ngo Huyen in the Cathedral District.

- **KOTO:** One delicious meal at the flagship restaurant of this nonprofit, which aims to uplift disadvantaged Vietnamese youth, and you'll understand why half the kitchens in Hanoi are staffed by KOTO grads.

chao suon

bun cha

Best Hotels

- **Hanoi Guesthouse:** This charming home away from home welcomes guests with a cozy common area, friendly staff, and well-appointed rooms.

- **Golden Time Hostel 3:** This small guesthouse makes for an excellent budget option amid the hustle and bustle of downtown Hanoi.

- **Hanoi La Siesta Diamond Hotel:** For high-end service at a mid-range price, this hotel sets a high bar for Hanoian hospitality and boasts, among other things, an on-site spa and a penthouse restaurant.

- **Hanoi Backpackers':** For the lively backpacker set, Hanoi Backpackers' offers clean beds and ample opportunities to make friends with other like-minded travelers.

cyclos awaiting passengers outside the Sofitel Legend Metropole

- **Sofitel Legend Metropole:** The capital's most famous luxury hotel, the Metropole has welcomed everyone from Charlie Chaplin to Jane Fonda during its many years of operation.

Hanoi La Siesta Diamond Hotel

Hanoi

Look for ★ to find recommended
sights, activities, dining, and lodging.

Highlights

★ **Ho Chi Minh Mausoleum:** Pay a visit to Vietnam's most revered national hero, embalmed and at peace under glass in a blocky, Soviet-style mausoleum (page 28).

★ **Temple of Literature:** A long series of lacquered pavilions and spacious courtyards, lotus ponds, and stone stelae, this Confucian temple marks the site of Vietnam's first university (page 33).

★ **Vietnam Museum of Ethnology:** Learn all there is to know about Vietnam's 54 ethnic groups, from the Kinh of the coast to the H'mong, Thai, Gia Rai, and scores of other lesser-known minorities that populate the country's mountainous interior (page 36).

★ **Minority Villages:** Whether perched on the steep cliffs of the Hoang Lien mountain range or sheltered by lush green river valleys, Sapa's minority villages are a world apart from the rest of the country (page 86).

★ **Mount Fansipan:** Reach the "Roof of Indochina" via a long, action-packed ascent that winds through clouds and over limestone ridges to the summit of Vietnam's highest peak (page 92).

★ **Hoan Kiem Lake:** Take in the bustle and noise of downtown Hanoi from the shores of this legendary lake, where history and mythology meet (page 19).

The fertile, low-lying Red River Delta that surrounds Hanoi has been inhabited since prehistoric times.

Well before it became the capital of Vietnam, the region was used as an administrative and political center by the Chinese, who colonized Vietnam for a millennium-long stretch beginning in 208 BC. The city's official history began in AD 1010, when emperor Ly Thai To moved the capital from Hoa Lu north to a bend on the western bank of the Red River. Originally known as Thang Long ("ascending dragon"), the imperial citadel remained in this spot for centuries.

At the turn of the 19th century, emperor Gia Long, the first of the Nguyen Dynasty, moved his capital to Hue, situated at the center of the country. During much of the Nguyen Dynasty's reign, Hanoi served as a regional capital. It received its current moniker in 1831, courtesy of emperor Minh Mang, Gia Long's son and successor. The city later reclaimed its capital status in 1902, when the colonial French government chose it as the head of French Indochina. It continued to serve as the seat of power after Ho Chi Minh declared Vietnamese independence in 1945. Nine years later, the Geneva Accords of 1954 granted northern Vietnam to the Viet Minh, who carried out their political operations in the grand colonial buildings left behind by the French.

The American War ushered in darker days, with heavy bombing reducing large parts of the city to rubble. Long Bien Bridge saw routine bombardments, while Bach Mai Hospital was almost completely destroyed during the Christmas bombings of 1972. The damage to the city would take years to rebuild. After the war, Hanoi struggled to regain its footing, through Vietnam's 1979 border war with China and the poor economic policies that followed reunification. When the country's *doi moi* reforms were enacted,

Opener: changing of the guard at Ho Chi Minh Mausoleum; flower vendor.
Opposite: Sapa rice terraces. **Above:** Buddha statue at Tran Quoc Pagoda.

allowing for greater economic freedom, Vietnam began to blossom into the country that it is today, bringing Hanoi out of its misery and back on the path to prosperity.

PLANNING YOUR TIME

Hanoi is no more than a three-day affair, thanks to its compact size, allowing visitors to cover plenty of ground in a short time. For additional adventures, such as Perfume Pagoda or Tam Coc, set aside an extra day. Trips to Sapa require as few as two days or as many as five, if you have time to spare.

Most museums are closed on Mondays, and many pagodas close for at least two hours for lunch. Sightsee in the mornings, when more of the city's attractions are open.

Weather conditions in Hanoi are different from the tropical temperatures of the lower half of the country. Between November and February, Hanoi gets cold, with a steady mist and temperatures 50-60°F. Conditions become more pleasant around March and stay that way until the end of May, when temperatures start to rise. The heat reaches unbearable, sweltering temps in August, before another brief period of mild weather in September and October.

ORIENTATION

Hanoi is divvied up into 12 districts, 17 communes, and one hamlet, though most travelers stick to the downtown districts and the areas just beyond.

Hoan Kiem District is home to the eponymous Hoan Kiem Lake, Hanoi's most famous landmark and a useful point of reference when navigating the city. Hoan Kiem is comprised of the bustling **Old Quarter,** where much of the city's commercial activity takes place, the posh **French Quarter,** and, along its western side, the **Cathedral District.** Along with picturesque St. Joseph's Cathedral, the Cathedral District houses cheap backpacker accommodations and trendy boutiques.

Northwest of Hoan Kiem, **Ba Dinh District** is where many of the capital's 20th-century historical sights are situated.

North of these downtown districts, **Tay Ho (West Lake)** is more upscale, with a residential feel and plenty of high-end shops and restaurants.

Hanoi's streets are winding and narrow, with names that change several times over the course of a mile. There are plenty of English-speaking residents downtown who can help to point you in the right direction. The city's public bus system is well-organized and affordable, with wide coverage and frequent service downtown and in other tourist-driven areas. *Xe om* and taxis are abundant and businesses are well-marked with street addresses.

Hanoi

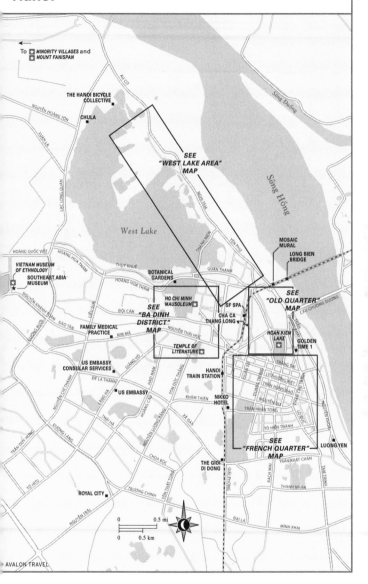

To ✚ MINORITY VILLAGES and
✚ MOUNT FANISPAN

THE HANOI BICYCLE COLLECTIVE

CHULA

SEE "WEST LAKE AREA" MAP

Song Hồng

West Lake

MOSAIC MURAL
LONG BIEN BRIDGE

HOANG QUOC VIET

VIETNAM MUSEUM OF ETHNOLOGY
SOUTHEAST ASIA MUSEUM

BOTANICAL GARDENS

HO CHI MINH MAUSOLEUM

SF SPA
CHA CA THANG LONG

SEE "OLD QUARTER" MAP

SEE "BA DINH DISTRICT" MAP

HOAN KIEM LAKE
GOLDEN TIME 1

FAMILY MEDICAL PRACTICE

TEMPLE OF LITERATURE

US EMBASSY CONSULAR SERVICES

HANOI TRAIN STATION

US EMBASSY

NIKKO HOTEL

SEE "FRENCH QUARTER" MAP

LUONG YEN

THE GIOI DI DONG

ROYAL CITY

0   0.5 mi

0   0.5 km

AVALON TRAVEL

Old Quarter

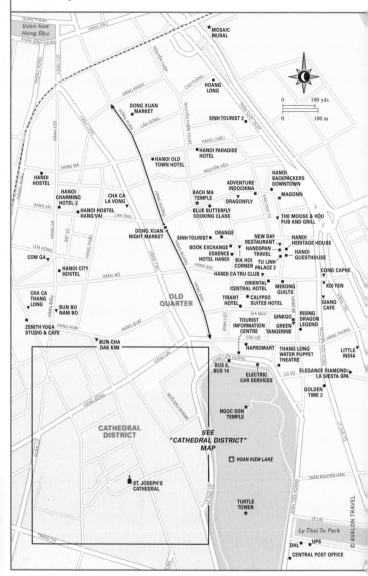

Sights

Hanoi's attractions span the entirety of its illustrious history, covering everything from imperial relics to colonial grandeur, the Communist revolution, and beyond. Scores of age-old pagodas dot the downtown neighborhoods, rubbing shoulders with crumbling art-deco architecture, a pair of legendary lakes, a few blocky Soviet-style buildings, and several museums that showcase the best of Hanoi's art, history, and culture.

This is the kind of place in which the journey rivals the destination. Rather than hop in a cab to the Temple of Literature, enlist the services of a cyclo driver or head for Ba Dinh District on foot. Even if it takes an extra hour and a few wrong turns, exploring the city this way brings its vibrancy to life.

SIGHTS

OLD QUARTER

A teeming, tight-knit neighborhood barely contained by the tiny streets north of Hoan Kiem Lake, the historic Old Quarter is bright, chaotic, and fun. Hanoi's most visited commercial district, it has been in business for centuries and holds its own amid the recent crop of shopping malls and high-end stores that have sprung up elsewhere in town. Throngs of shoppers, street vendors, motorbikes, and storefronts crowd the narrow one-way streets and bustling alleys of this dense neighborhood, which functions like a large central market.

★ Hoan Kiem Lake

The focal point of the Old Quarter, **Hoan Kiem Lake** (corner of Dinh Tien Hoang and Le Thai To) is tranquility surrounded by chaos, its placid water ringed by traffic. Legend has it that emperor Le Thai To received a magical sword from the heavens, which he used to drive the Ming Chinese out of Vietnam in the early 15th century. After his victory, the king was rowing on

Turtle Tower, Hoan Kiem Lake

A Long Weekend in Hanoi

While the thousand-year-old city holds plenty of history, the most captivating moment in Hanoi is the present. Follow this three-day itinerary to explore the storied past of the capital while experiencing the best of a modern-day Vietnamese metropolis at the same time. Taxis, *xe om,* and public buses are widely available, but traveling by foot allows you to feel Hanoi's topsy-turvy energy.

Day 1

Follow the locals and start your day early with breakfast at the hotel or a piping hot bowl of pho on the street. Any good Hanoian adventure begins with a trip to **Hoan Kiem Lake,** the epicenter of town, followed by nearby **Ngoc Son Temple.** From the northern edge of the water, you should be able to enlist the services of a cyclo driver, who will ferry you around the narrow, chaotic streets of the **Old Quarter** in order to witness the city in full swing. If you're up for it, walking is also an option, though the uninitiated will find downtown Hanoi's streets hectic. There are ample opportunities for shopping along **Hang Gai** and around the web of streets north of the lake.

Around lunchtime, you'll want to head toward **St. Joseph's Cathedral** on the western flank of the lake. Swing by the **Le Thai To Monument** and **Nam Huong Temple,** overlooking Hoan Kiem on the way, before cutting in toward the church. If you're feeling peckish, tuck into a savory bowl of *chao suon* (rice porridge), served daily in the alley near the cathedral, or visit the clutch of chic international restaurants sitting in the shadow of its towers. Nearby, **Hanoi Social Club** offers a tasty, unique alternative. Finish off your midday meal in true Vietnamese form at one of the cafés around St. Joseph's. Several cheap local **street cafés** offer affordable coffee and tea and plastic stools to perch on.

In the afternoon, make your way toward **Hoa Lo Prison** for a bit of history before turning east toward the top-notch **Vietnamese Women's Museum.** As the day winds down, stroll and shop along trendy **Trang Tien** street or pay a visit to the **Opera House** nearby. Enjoy a sunset drink from the terrace bar of the **Press Club** or grab a seat street-side in the artsy front room of **Tadioto.**

Dinner is left up to you, as you'll probably want to hop on a *xe om* or grab a cab to reach one of Hanoi's more authentic local meals. **Ngon** makes a great choice, as do the *cha ca* (pan-fried fish) restaurants a few blocks north of the lake. If you're up for some live entertainment in the evening, the band at **Minh's Jazz Club** puts on a nightly show, as do a rotating list of acts at **Swing.**

the lake when a massive turtle appeared, took the sword from his belt, and sank back into the depths below. Le Thai To realized that the blade had been returned to its original owner, thus the lake became known as Hoan Kiem ("Lake of the Returned Sword"). On a small island near the southern end of the water is **Turtle Tower,** a structure built in 1886 to honor Le Thai To. During the French occupation, the tower held a small version of the Statue of Liberty, but it was destroyed when the city was wrested from French rule.

The lake and its surrounding park are a meeting place for locals. On weekends, the city government closes the roads around Hoan Kiem to

Day 2

You'll want to get an early jump on your second day, as the sights west of Hoan Kiem Lake require time and patience. In the morning, hop on a bus from the northern edge of the lake to **Ba Dinh Square,** where you can queue up for a visit to **Ho Chi Minh Mausoleum.** Dress respectfully; the rules are strict here. After you've made your way through the procession, you can snap photos of the square or head back toward Uncle Ho's famous **stilt house** and the **One Pillar Pagoda.** From here, those interested in learning more about Vietnam's war-related history should chart a course for the **Military History Museum,** while travelers who'd rather explore a local neighborhood can wander down the maze of alleys that precede **B-52 Lake.**

Around noon, head south toward the **Temple of Literature.** Just across the street, **KOTO** is a busy lunchtime destination and great spot for a meal. Once you've paid a visit to the temple, you can wander back to the Old Quarter along Nguyen Thai Hoc, shopping as you go, or spend an hour at the **Museum of Fine Arts** nearby. Take the rest of the afternoon to relax and then set off again in the early evening for any one of Hanoi's local *bia hoi* (freshly brewed light beer) shops. The area around *bia hoi* **corner** in the Old Quarter offers a host of affordable street-side dining options as well as a collection of lively dance floors and laid-back hangouts.

Day 3

Spend the morning at the **Museum of Ethnology** west of downtown. Because it's a trek and the museum itself is extensive, you'll want to allow ample time to explore the grounds, which include several outdoor replicas of traditional minority houses. Head back toward West Lake around noon for a roadside bowl of *bun cha* (grilled meat and rice noodles in fish sauce) on Hang Than street.

After lunch, walk over to **Quan Thanh Temple** before taking a leisurely stroll along **West Lake.** If you're up for it, you can follow the edge of **Truc Bach** lake or simply head straight to **Tran Quoc Pagoda.** It's possible to grab a coffee near here and admire **West Lake** from this vantage point, or to visit the bar at the **Pan Pacific Hanoi** for a more upscale environment. Grab dinner at bustling **Xoi Yen** in the Old Quarter before catching a cultural performance in the evening. Both the **water puppet theater** near Hoan Kiem Lake and a pair of *ca tru* (ancient chamber music) troupes hold regular shows throughout the week.

traffic, transforming the area into a lively pedestrian street full of kids zipping about on inline skates, vendors selling snacks, and impromptu dance and musical performances.

Ngoc Son Temple

On a small islet near the northern end of Hoan Kiem Lake, the grounds of **Ngoc Son Temple** (Dinh Tien Hoang, 7am-6pm Mon.-Fri., 7am-9pm Sat.-Sun., VND30,000, free for children under 15) originally served as a fishing dock for emperor Le Thanh Tong during the 15th century. Though the structure you see wasn't built until 1865, this small patch of land once housed a palace and, later, a pagoda. Ngoc Son Temple combines its Buddhist past with Confucian and Taoist influences.

The temple's front half is dedicated to Quan Cong, a loyal and courageous Chinese general of the Shu Han Dynasty. A flurry of red, black, and gold lacquerwork encircles his three-tiered altar, laden with fruit offerings. Alongside Quan Cong's beloved red horse is La To, a practitioner of traditional medicine and Taoist spirit.

Vietnamese general Tran Hung Dao presides over the latter portion of the temple, tucked behind a high altar. Tran Hung Dao is credited with the defeat of two Mongol invasions, most famously in 1288, when he drove off Kublai Khan and his army after impaling their ships with wooden spikes. He is worshipped as one of the country's collective ancestors.

Ngoc Son houses a small exhibit on the turtles of Hoan Kiem Lake. The lake's last living turtle passed away in 2016.

Leading to Ngoc Son's entrance gate is a bright red footbridge, a popular photo spot. On the far side of the path, look out for a relief of a tortoise on the left, carrying Le Thai To's famous sword. The area before Ngoc Son boasts nice views of Turtle Tower and the lake.

Hanoi Heritage House

Acting as both a tourist information center and an example of traditional Hanoian architecture, the **Hanoi Heritage House** (87 Ma May, 8:30am-noon and 1:30pm-5pm daily, VND10,000) is a long and narrow building stocked with a variety of Vietnamese handicrafts and helpful English explanations of each item's origin. The house hails from the late 19th century and is punctuated by a small, roofless courtyard, which provides ventilation.

Both levels are stocked with souvenirs, including Dong Ho folk paintings and ceramics, stone carvings, and other traditional wares. While it can feel like a shop, there's no pressure to purchase.

At the front desk are a few books outlining the history of the neighborhood and its many small streets, as well as their former purposes. Curious travelers can ask questions about the city.

Bach Ma Temple

The oldest temple in Hanoi, 11th-century **Bach Ma Temple** (76 Hang Buom, 8am-11am and 2pm-5pm Tues.-Sun., free) may be modest in size, but through its humble gates are inner walls drenched in red and gold, floor-to-ceiling lacquerwork, intricate paintings, and masterful woodwork. This tranquil hall honors deity Long Do, the chief of Hanoi's first settlement, who lived during the 4th century and is believed to have reappeared several times throughout Vietnamese history, particularly during conflicts with the Chinese, as a protector of the city and its people. Since he would sometimes appear in the form of a white horse, it is fitting that the temple's name translates to white horse. A large statue of a bright white stallion stands at the center of the building, surrounded by offerings and massive, gilded ironwood columns. Overhead, Bach Ma's collection of lintels (large lacquered wooden panels) featuring Chinese inscriptions, bear phrases such as "Thang Long's Guardian to the East" and "Indomitable Spirit of Heaven and Earth."

Temple caretakers typically break for lunch at midday. Visitors who turn up on the 1st or 15th of a lunar month are free to visit from morning to night, as these are special days in Vietnamese culture.

Long Bien Bridge

Long Bien Bridge (east of Tran Nhat Duat), a weathered iron structure, holds a special place in Hanoi's history. Completed in 1902 by French architects, the bridge was originally named after Indochina's governor general, Paul Doumer. It played a key role in both the Franco-Vietnam and American Wars. During the Viet Minh's fight against colonialism, rice and other supplies traveled across Long Bien to the troops at Dien Bien Phu, who defeated their French enemies in 1954. Through the 1960s and '70s the bridge served as a crucial link between Hanoi and the port city of Haiphong. As the only route across the Red River, Long Bien was bombed heavily during the American War and had to be rebuilt in 1973.

Only pedestrians and two-wheeled vehicles are permitted on the bridge. Nearby Chuong Duong Bridge serves as a link for trucks and other large vehicles.

Mosaic Mural

Running beneath Long Bien Bridge along Tran Nhat Duat, Hanoi's **mosaic mural** began as a project to commemorate the city's 1,000-year anniversary. It spans almost 2.5 miles along the western bank of the Red River, making it the longest ceramic wall in the world. Both local and foreign artists took part in the mosaic's creation, combining abstract pieces from international artists with several prominent Vietnamese symbols, such as a mosaic version of a Dong Son drum head and the ever-popular giant turtle of Hoan Kiem Lake carrying a sword on its back.

CATHEDRAL DISTRICT
St. Joseph's Cathedral

An imposing structure amid the narrow houses and one-room shops of downtown Hanoi, **St. Joseph's Cathedral** (40 Nha Chung, tel. 04/3825-4424, 5am-7am and 7pm-9pm daily, free) is one of the city's more recognizable landmarks, its pair of faded Gothic bell towers presiding over a small clearing just west of Hoan Kiem Lake. Originally the site of Bao Thien Pagoda, a Buddhist hall of worship dating as far back as the city itself, the church, built to resemble Paris's Notre Dame Cathedral, opened in 1886 to a devout French parish. St. Joseph's remained open until the end of the American War, when the Communist government forbade religious gatherings. The cathedral reopened its doors in the early 1990s.

The modest square before the church, ringed by cafés and boutiques,

Cathedral District

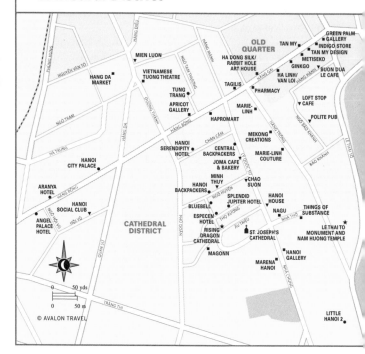

boasts a statue of Mother Mary and is often busy in the late afternoons with students and locals. Though the front doors are usually closed, there is a side door by which visitors can enter to glimpse the brilliant red, white, and gold interior; most prefer to just take in the building from outside. Visitors can drop by the cathedral's English-language mass on Sundays at 11:30am if they feel so inclined.

Le Thai To Monument and Nam Huong Temple

Overlooking Hoan Kiem Lake, the towering **Le Thai To Monument** (Le Thai To, 8am-5pm daily, free) commemorates Le Thai To, the emperor who played a pivotal role in Vietnam's history and mythology. Also known as Le Loi, this 15th-century king defeated Chinese invaders with the help of a magical sword. Topped by a small statue of the emperor, the 1896 monument is well-preserved and vibrant, bordered by an array of blooms and large shade trees. A sturdy pavilion obscures the base of the memorial where incense and other offerings are laid.

Behind the statue, **Nam Huong Temple** honors the emperor and a handful of other deified citizens. It once served as a popular gathering place for writers, poets, and scholars, moving to its present location at the turn of the 20th century. While the temple is small (the width of the room is about five paces), the emperor's altar holds a riot of colorful offerings, decorative statues, and a few lacquered wooden tablets.

FRENCH QUARTER
Opera House

The grand old **Opera House** (1 Trang Tien, tel. 04/3933-0113, www.hanoioperahouse.org.vn) is a stately structure overlooking the frenzied August Revolution Square. The theater, a yellow-and-white behemoth built in the colonial style, took a decade to complete, first opening its doors in 1911. Back then, only European performers were invited onto the stage, and French colonists made up most of the audience. By 1940, Vietnamese citizens were able to rent out the massive hall, modeled after Paris's own opera house. When politics took center stage in 1945 and Vietnam declared its independence from the French, Hanoi's Opera House served as a meeting venue for gatherings of the new government.

Performances take place year-round. The opulent theater seats 598 spectators over three levels. Though visitors aren't permitted to wander around indoors, the exterior is worth a look while you're in the French Quarter.

National Museum of History and Revolutionary Museum

Housed in the former Louis Finot Museum, the **National Museum of History** (1 Pham Ngu Lao, tel. 04/3824-1384, www.baotanglichsu.vn, 8am-noon and 1:30pm-5pm daily, VND40,000) showcases over 200,000 artifacts, documents, and historic relics. The main building is devoted to ancient civilizations such as the Sa Huynh, Oc Eo, and Champa, along with northern Vietnam's Dong Son, a culture which existed roughly in 1000 BC-AD 100 and whose large bronze drums are a symbol of Vietnam. Scores of artifacts (stone implements, pottery, and jewelry) occupy the downstairs level, while the museum's upper floor packs in several centuries of dynastic

the grand Opera House

French Quarter

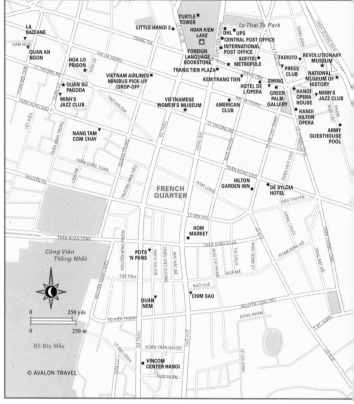

rule, from the Dinh and Le eras of the AD 900s to Vietnam's last emperors, the Nguyen dynasty, whose ornate everyday items, from mother-of-pearl inlaid dressers to enamel jars, detailed ceramics, and vibrant lacquerware take up a display to themselves.

Despite a fair amount of English signage throughout the building, a lack of general historical information can leave non-Vietnamese speakers adrift.

Where the National Museum of History leaves off—with the text of Uncle Ho's famous declaration of independence, given at Ba Dinh Square on September 2, 1945—the **Revolutionary Museum** across the street picks up, with a smaller range of documents, artifacts, and propaganda from the Franco-Vietnam and American Wars.

Entry to both museums is included in the ticket price, and visitors can spread out their visits over more than one day. There is a camera fee (VND15,000) to take photos within the museums. Both museums are closed the first Monday of the month.

Vietnamese Women's Museum

One of Hanoi's better offerings, the **Vietnamese Women's Museum** (36 Ly Thuong Kiet, tel. 04/3825-9936, www.baotangphunu.org.vn, 8am-5pm daily, VND30,000) takes a comprehensive look at the country's female citizens. Permanent exhibits cover everything from marriage and birth customs to family life, the crucial role of women in Vietnamese history, and the varied traditions practiced by ethnic minorities, all with ample English signage. A handful of temporary displays also pass through the modern, three-story building. The museum's clear organization places it a cut above many others in the city.

Hoa Lo Prison

In the heart of the French Quarter is a small portion of **Hoa Lo Prison** (Hoa Lo and Hai Ba Trung, tel. 04/3824-6358, www.hoalo.vn, 8am-5pm daily, VND30,000, free for children under 15), the infamous jail that once housed thousands of Vietnamese revolutionaries during colonialism and, later, American prisoners of war. While most of the original complex has been demolished, the remainder of Hoa Lo serves as a museum, documenting its history and the struggles of its inmates.

Built by the French at the end of the 19th century, the facility then known as the Maison Centrale quickly surpassed its original 450-prisoner capacity, overflowing with nationalist Vietnamese who had rebelled against colonial rule. As many as 2,000 inmates were crammed in at one time, making for dismal conditions on top of the torture doled out by French prison guards. The museum holds ample evidence of these transgressions, including life-sized mannequins of Vietnamese prisoners, lined up and shackled at the feet, as well as a guillotine used by the colonial government during the early 20th century. Following the Franco-Vietnam and American Wars, several of Hoa Lo's inmates went on to serve as high-ranking officials in the Vietnamese Communist Party.

plaque in Hoa Lo Prison

From the 1960s onward, the prison earned a new nickname. Dubbed the "Hanoi Hilton" by American soldiers, the complex was re-purposed by north Vietnamese forces for prisoners of war. Here, the story fractures into two separate accounts: that of its captives—including U.S. Senator John McCain, who spent over five years at Hoa Lo—who recall torture and brutality; and that of the Vietnamese government, which paints a rosy portrait of life on the inside, complete with Christmas dinners and organized sports.

The museum has a small memorial to its Vietnamese prisoners at the back of the complex. Visitors are free to wander the exhibits at their leisure. Skip the information booklets on sale at the ticket booth, as much of their text is featured on signs throughout the museum.

Quan Su Pagoda

Just south of Hoa Lo Prison, the wide yellow **Quan Su Pagoda** (Chua Quan Su, 73 Quan Su, 8am-11am and 1pm-4pm daily, free) is one of Hanoi's most popular centers of worship and home to the Buddhist Association of Vietnam. Though it's not the city's oldest or even its most decorated pagoda, Quan Su, also known as the Ambassador's Pagoda, began in the 15th century as a guesthouse for visiting emissaries from Buddhist countries and has only grown since then. The current building was constructed in 1942 and features a dimly lit congregation of Buddha effigies on the main altar, a many-armed Quan Am, and a small section dedicated to local martyrs. Despite its downtown location, the pagoda courtyard is a peaceful place most days, though dozens gather here during religious festivals and holidays. For anything and everything Buddhism-related, check out the surrounding shops, where scores of religious books, relics, and other goods are sold.

BA DINH DISTRICT

You could easily pass a day in Ba Dinh District, where many of Hanoi's most prominent historical monuments cluster together south of West Lake. Though these sights focus on Vietnam's 20th-century history, much of it war-related or steeped in Communism, there are a few other worthy attractions in the area, such as the city's Museum of Fine Arts and the centuries-old Temple of Literature.

★ Ho Chi Minh Mausoleum

A stark stone cube occupying the western edge of massive Ba Dinh Square, the **Ho Chi Minh Mausoleum** (Ba Dinh Square, tel. 04/3845-5128, www.bqllang.gov.vn, 7:30am-10:30am Tues.-Thurs., 7:30am-11am Sat.-Sun. summer, 8am-11am Tues.-Thurs., 8am-11:30am Sat.-Sun. winter, free) bears only the words "President Ho Chi Minh" on its exterior. Guarded day and night by police in crisp white uniforms, this is perhaps one of Hanoi's most bizarre sights. On most mornings, dozens of local visitors line up to catch a glimpse of their leader's embalmed body. The swift, two-line procession

Ba Dinh District

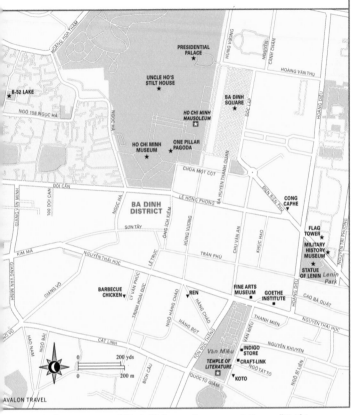

moves indoors past one of Uncle Ho's most famous quotations—"Nothing is more precious than independence and freedom"—before gliding in a semi-circle around the body and back outside. Upon his death in 1969, Uncle Ho requested to be cremated and his ashes scattered in three parts throughout the north, south, and central regions of Vietnam, a wish that was obviously ignored.

Respectful dress is a must. Strict silence is observed indoors and no photography or camera equipment is permitted beyond the security checkpoint at the southern end of Ba Dinh Square, nor is the use of cell phones. Once you enter the line, it moves quickly, letting out on the opposite side of the building, where you can collect your electronics and carry on, either back out to the street or to any one of the Uncle Ho-related sights nearby.

Presidential Palace and Ho Chi Minh's Stilt House

Behind Ho Chi Minh's mausoleum, the **Presidential Palace** (1 Bach Thao, tel. 04/0804-4287, 7:30am-11am and 1:30pm-4pm daily summer,

8am-11am and 1:30pm-4pm daily winter, closed Mon. afternoons, VND25,000) and his famous **stilt house** are remnants of both the French colonial government and its Communist successors. The bright, sunflower-hued palace, once home to the governor general of Indochina, served as both a private residence and administrative building for the colonial powers. Following Vietnam's independence, it was expected that Uncle Ho, as president, would move into the massive house. Instead, he converted the building into a solely political and administrative structure. The president made his home in a smaller structure nearby, now known as the 54 House, named after the year in which he moved in. This residence was short-lived.

At the same time, Ho Chi Minh commissioned a wooden stilt house, built in the style of Vietnam's ethnic minorities, where he lived for most of his remaining days. The modest, two-story building features an open ground floor, used for business, and sparsely furnished living quarters upstairs. The nearby fish pond and mango trees occupied much of the president's down time. A third and equally humble residence sits on the far side of the stilt house, completed in 1967 out of concern for Uncle Ho's well-being, as American bombs began to rain down on Hanoi in greater numbers. Ho Chi Minh passed away here in September 1969.

Visitors can't access the Presidential Palace, which opens only for visiting heads of state. At the stilt house, you can only observe the upper floor of the building on an adjacent platform. A handful of artifacts are on display, including a few gifts presented to Ho Chi Minh by world leaders, as well as three gleaming antique cars used by the late president for travel, two of which were donated by the Soviet Union.

For more insight into this area, request a free English-speaking guide at the ticket booth. Guides are primarily university students who have taken the job to practice their language skills, so don't be surprised if the tour isn't terribly thorough.

Ho Chi Minh Mausoleum

The gargantuan, lotus-shaped **Ho Chi Minh Museum** (19 Ngoc Ha, tel. 04/3846-3757, 8am-11:30am and 2pm-4pm Tues.-Thurs. and Sat.-Sun, 8am-11:30am Mon. and Fri.) is not the only Ho Chi Minh-related museum in Vietnam, but it is hands-down the biggest, packed with thousands of historical documents and artifacts, photographs, and exhibits on the life and achievements of the revolutionary leader. Over two floors, the museum's displays cover much of Uncle Ho's time abroad and his involvement in politics in France, China, and the United States, before his return to take up arms against the French. While there is heavy-handed Communist glorification and the English signage fails to offer big-picture synopses of Ho Chi Minh's life, it's a worthwhile attraction for history buffs. Before visiting, read even just a few paragraphs about Ho Chi Minh for a better appreciation of the exhibits.

One Pillar Pagoda

The short, squat **One Pillar Pagoda (Chua Mot Cot)** (6am-11am and 2pm-6pm daily, free) is dwarfed by the grand Communist monuments nearby, but it bears an interesting origin story. Standing at 13 feet high, the modest shrine, dedicated to Quan Am, is believed to date back to AD 1049, during the reign of emperor Ly Thai Tong. The legend goes that the inspiration for the pagoda came to the emperor in a dream, but there are conflicting versions of what the vision contained. Some say that the emperor dreamed of Quan Am sitting on a lotus blossom, holding a baby boy in her arms. The emperor, who wished for a son, became a father shortly thereafter and erected the monument as a thank-you to Quan Am. Given that Ly Thai Tong's son was born a few years before he ascended the throne in 1028, it doesn't seem likely that this version is correct.

The second version says that the emperor dreamed of Quan Am bringing him to a lotus lamp. Ly Thai Tong's mandarins worried that it was a

altar outside of Dien Huu Pagoda

bad omen. In an effort to counteract this negativity, the emperor commissioned the pagoda, paying homage to Quan Am.

The pagoda has undergone countless restorations and was rebuilt in 1249 and again in 1954, after the French destroyed it. Opposite the small shrine, **Dien Huu Pagoda** is a newer, more colorful building filled with a collection of statues and shrines that pairs nicely with a stroll up the steps of One Pillar.

The pagoda's proximity to Ho Chi Minh Museum and Ho Chi Minh Mausoleum makes it a frequent stop for visitors in Ba Dinh.

B-52 Lake

B-52 Lake (Ho Huu Tiep) (Ngo 158 Ngoc Ha or Ngo 55 Hoang Hoa Tham) sits amid a sleepy residential neighborhood, all but forgotten. Faded into Hanoi's everyday bustle, its tepid green waters serve as the backdrop for morning commutes, daily garbage collection, and the comings and goings of street vendors. Stretching up from the lake's surface is a stark reminder of the not-so-distant past: the mangled husk of a B-52 fighter jet, shot down during the 1972 Christmas bombings that rocked northern Vietnam. While much of the nearby landscape has changed, the lake remains frozen in time, a modest but powerful visual.

B-52 Lake elicits mixed reactions. For history and war buffs, it's a worthwhile stop paired with a visit to Ho Chi Minh Mausoleum and other surrounding sights. There is a simple plaque that stands at the near end of the water, and the plane's wreckage is surprisingly small.

To reach B-52 Lake you'll have to navigate several small alleys. Keep an eye out for signs that read "Ho B-52" or "Ho Huu Tiep" (the original name of the lake), as there are no English signs.

Military History Museum

The national **Military History Museum** (28A Dien Bien Phu, tel.

the Military History Museum

04/3823-4264, www.btlsqsvn.org.vn, 8am-11:30am and 1pm-4pm Tues.-Thurs. and Sat.-Sun., VND40,000) gathers various artifacts from Vietnam's two most prominent 20th-century wars, against French and American forces, within a bright white building. The indoor displays feature photos of the destruction that occurred.

The museum's outdoor exhibits provide more intrigue, with a sizable collection of military aircraft and ammunition, including one of the famous tanks that crashed through the gates of Saigon's Independence Palace on April 30, 1975, ending the American War. The museum highlights the cunning and resilience of a nation that, equipped with few resources, took on one of the world's most powerful armies and prevailed.

The grounds of the Military History Museum house Hanoi's red brick **Flag Tower,** a remnant of the imperial era built by emperor Gia Long in 1812. While it is possible to enter the tower and take the steps up to the highest of its platforms, those who pass on the museum can still see the monument from the street, and the photos are just as good, if not better, from here. The museum charges a camera fee (VND30,000), which includes the outdoor exhibits.

★ Temple of Literature

Hanoi's **Temple of Literature** (58 Quoc Tu Giam, tel. 04/3845-2917, 8am-5pm daily winter, 7:30am-5:30pm daily summer, VND20,000) hearkens back to AD 1070, when emperor Ly Thanh Tong ordered the construction of this temple complex. In 1076, emperor Ly Nhan Tong inaugurated Vietnam's first university, Quoc Tu Giam, on the long, rectangular grounds. The professors were court-appointed mandarins, who taught lessons on Confucianism, administration, literature, and poetry.

While the university no longer stands, its grounds still hold an attractive garden, several lotus ponds, and the temple itself. Outside the main gate, a pair of stone engravings (in traditional Vietnamese characters)

Temple of Literature

commands visitors to dismount from their horses. Through the imposing front door is a pleasant garden, filled with bright red flowers and frangipani trees. Lanterns line the central walkway that leads to the Khue Van pavilion, built in 1805, a tall, ornamental structure topped with bright red lacquered wood.

The temple's most famous attractions rest upon 82 giant stone tortoises, meant to symbolize wisdom and longevity. The 82 stelae honor Quoc Tu Giam's 1,304 doctoral graduates. While you aren't allowed to wander through the rows of stelae, you can see the stone tablets up close.

The courtyard before the Temple of Literature once held altars for 72 of the most respected students to study under Confucius and, later, Chu Van An, a 13th-century scholar considered the father of Vietnamese education. The altar has been replaced with souvenir vendors hawking incense and a few interesting handicrafts.

The temple itself is divided into two sections. Under the first roof, a high altar sits in the open air, flanked by tortoise and crane statues. Everything from the ironwood columns to the gold Chinese inscriptions shines with a heavy lacquer, and incense fills the air. Beyond the high door—used to ensure entrants bow their heads in respect—is a large statue of Confucius and his disciples, dressed in lavish robes. A gold-plated ceramic tortoise sits to the left, while several smaller altars line the outskirts of the room.

Behind the temple are the original university grounds, now known as Thai Hoc courtyard. Completed in 2000, this area is dedicated to three Vietnamese emperors: Ly Thanh Tong, responsible for the original temple's construction; Ly Nhan Tong, founder of the national university; and Le Thanh Tong, the ruler who commissioned the first of the stelae.

While signage within the temple complex is fairly sparse, visitors can hire a guide (VND100,000) at the ticket booth or buy the information booklet (VND8,000). Though nothing beats a knowledgeable and enthusiastic guide, the booklet provides insight and historical background for a fraction of the cost.

WEST LAKE AREA
West Lake

North of the Old Quarter, **West Lake (Ho Tay)** is Hanoi's largest body of water and a center for the city's wealthier residents. Ringed with luxury hotels and high-end restaurants, the lake once served as the northern frontier for Thang Long citadel. Of the legends related to the lake's origin, the most popular one goes that the area was once a forest, terrorized by a nine-tailed demon, which Lac Long Quan, original leader of the Vietnamese people, drowned in the waters of West Lake. Another story goes that an 11th-century monk by the name of Khong Lo traveled to China to aid the emperor and, as a reward for his services, carried home large amounts of bronze. He used that bronze to make a bell with a sound so powerful that it confused a golden calf, who mistook the noise for its mother calling and, in his hurry to find her, created the deep rut that would form West Lake.

A narrow strip of land runs between West Lake and small **Truc Bach.** Though these two bodies of water were originally one, the southern lake received its own name after the completion of the Co Ngu causeway, upon which Tran Quoc Pagoda now sits. Truc Bach is remembered in Vietnam's war history as the site where, on October 26, 1967, American pilot John McCain parachuted into the water after his plane was shot down. Vietnamese civilians rescued the pilot before turning him in to Hoa Lo, where he spent over five years as a prisoner of war. A plaque near the lakeshore commemorates the event.

A trip to West Lake provides plenty of peace and quiet, and the lake boasts a 10-mile road around its shoreline, making for a scenic stroll or bike ride.

Tran Quoc Pagoda

One of Hanoi's oldest houses of worship, the **Tran Quoc Pagoda** (Thanh Nien/Co Ngu causeway, 7:30am-11:30am and 1:30pm-6:30pm daily, free) dates back to the 6th century, when its first incarnation was built on the banks of the Red River during the reign of emperor Ly Nam De. Its current home looks out over the gentle waters of West Lake and provides lovely views of the surrounding area.

Through a large yellow gate, the front half of Tran Quoc houses a collection of colorful stupas dwarfed by the 11-tiered tower at their center, which houses a ring of white Buddha statues on all sides. From this courtyard, visitors are able to peek in on the pagoda's ancestral altars, which line the wall of a shallow room off to the right. Farther back, a larger

West Lake Area

HANOI ROCK CITY
NGÕ TÔ NGỌC VÂN
ZED'S THREADS • • JOMA
• VEGGY'S
VEN HO MOI
JUST MASSAGE •
TÂY HÔ
ĐẶNG THAI MAI
ĐẶNG THAI MAI
NGÕ 200 ÂU CƠ
ANNAM GOURMET/ INTERNATIONAL SOS
HANOI BICYCLE COLLECTIVE
QUONG AN
CLOM'S CLOSET •
ZEN SPA •
88 LOUNGE •
NGÕ 124 ÂU CƠ
TU HOA CONG CHUA
SAINT HONORE •
SHERATON HANOI •
INTERCONTINENTAL WEST LAKE •
THANG LOI POOL •
0   200 yds
0   200 m
West Lake
LÀNG YEN PHU
YEN PHU
NGHI TÀM
HIDDEN HANOI •
HANOI CLUB DRIVING RANGE •
SOFITEL PLAZA HANOI •
AN DUONG
TRAN QUOC PAGODA ★
THANH NIEN
QUAN THANH TEMPLE ★
TRUC BACH
NGỌ XÁ
HANOI COOKING CENTRE/BOOKWORM •
ĐẶNG TÁT
PHAN ĐÌNH PHÙNG
NGUYÊN BIÊU
TRÂN VŨ
CHÂU LONG
CỬA BẮC
NGUYÊN TRƯỜNG TỘ
NGUYÊN KHÁC HIÊU
HÀNG THAN
TÂN ÁP
HÀNG ĐẬU
QUÁN THÁNH
HOÀNG DIỆU
NGUYÊN TRI PHƯƠNG
HÒE NHAI
PHÓ ĐÚC CHÍNH
HÀNG ĐẬU
YÊN PHU
PHAN HUY ÍCH
HONG NGOC HOSPITAL •
MANZI ▼
54 TRADITIONS •
HOÈ NHAI
BUN CHA ▼
© AVALON TRAVEL

clearing houses a broad, leafy bodhi tree, gifted to the pagoda in 1959 by Indian president Rajendra Prasad. The bodhi tree carries special religious significance, as it was under this type of tree that the Sakyamuni Buddha attained enlightenment in India. Another altar sits indoors, dedicated to Buddha and piled high with fruit offerings and lacquered ornamentation.

Quan Thanh Temple

As old as Hanoi itself, **Quan Thanh Temple** (corner of Quan Thanh and Thanh Nien, sunrise-sunset daily, VND10,000) was built in the 11th century under the reign of emperor Ly Thai To. Sitting just below West Lake, the temple honors Huyen Thien Tran Vu, protector of the city's northern gate, one of four directional deities who were believed to guard the Thang Long citadel in Hanoi's earliest days. The existing temple dates back to the 19th century and houses several precious antiques, including a 12-foot, four-ton statue of Tran Vu, cast in 1677, that takes up the back wall, as well as an oddly shaped gong from the 17th or 18th century. Through the temple's high white gate, a pair of stone elephants guard the courtyard leading up to Tran Vu's altar, lined with benches and large shade trees. Inside, lacquered woodwork decorates much of the shrine, while a photocopied map hangs on one of the building's columns, illustrating the parameters of Thang Long citadel and Quan Thanh Temple around 1490.

★ Vietnam Museum of Ethnology

Though it's removed from the rest of Hanoi's attractions, the **Vietnam Museum of Ethnology** (Nguyen Van Huyen, tel. 04/3756-2193, www. vme.org.vn, 8:30am-5:30pm Tues.-Sun., VND40,000) is worth a jaunt out to the western suburbs of the city. Opened in 1997, the large, round building, modeled after a Dong Son bronze drum, features exhibits on all 54 of Vietnam's ethnic communities, from the Kinh, or Vietnamese, who make up roughly 86 percent of the country's population, to dozens

Chinese characters adorn the entrance of Quan Thanh Temple.

of minority groups, including the Cham, H'mong, Muong, Jarai, and Ede, many of whom live in the mountainous regions of northwestern and central Vietnam. Ample signage guides visitors through the museum's vivid and educational exhibits, which cover customs, traditional dress, religion, architecture, farming techniques, handicrafts, and rituals practiced by each ethnicity. A small section on the 2nd floor organizes interactive activities for younger visitors, including traditional games and crafts.

Behind the building, several examples of traditional architecture are on display, including a stilted Ede longhouse and the soaring pitched roof of a Bahnar communal house, standing at 62 feet tall. **Water puppet performances** (10am, 11:30am, 2:30pm, and 4pm) take place several times a day in the pond nearby.

The museum is home to a small bookshop and souvenir store, as well as a café, run by the Hoa Sua School, an organization that trains disadvantaged Vietnamese youth. Book guided tours (VND100,000) ahead of time by calling the museum. There is also a camera fee (VND50,000) to take photos within the museum grounds.

To the right of the museum entrance is a building that curates a collection of cultural items from across Southeast Asia. Though still very much in its infancy, the Southeast Asian arm of the ethnology museum will feature the same in-depth displays on customs, styles of dress, handicrafts, religions, and other facets of culture within Vietnam and its neighboring nations. It's worth a peek while you're here.

SIGHTSEEING TOURS

In a city as accessible as Hanoi, city tours aren't entirely necessary, as most travelers are able to hit their preferred points of interest alone. There are plenty of standard, generic city tours around town; skip these since they don't enhance your Hanoian experience. A handful of outfits in the capital excel at providing urban excursions with a more personal touch.

Vietnam Museum of Ethnology

Founded in 2006, **Hanoi Kids** (tel. 09/8327-8272, www.hanoikids.org, 9am-5pm daily) is a free, student-run tour service that pairs curious travelers with young Vietnamese hoping to practice their English. All guides participate in regular training sessions before hitting the town with their new foreign friends, and your only costs as a traveler are admission fees and transportation for you and your guide. With equal give and take, these young Hanoians are enthusiastic and outgoing, making the experience feel more like a friendly outing than a run-of-the-mill tour. Due to the popularity of the group, reserving a spot ahead of time is a must. The booking department at Hanoi Kids sometimes needs a reminder. Confirm your tour in advance and, if response seems slow, give the office a call and check in.

A popular and reliable operator for tours both in town and around northern Vietnam, **Adventure Indochina** (6 Ma May, tel. 04/6683-5539, www.adventureindochina.com, 8am-9pm daily) arranges trips to Ha Long Bay and Sapa in addition to running city tours of Hanoi, cyclo excursions, a one-day journey focused around the city's pagodas, and a tasty street food tour. Staff are knowledgeable and efficient, and prices tend toward the more affordable end of the spectrum.

Just over two miles north of the Old Quarter, **Hidden Hanoi** (147 Nghi Tam, tel. 09/1225-4045, www.hiddenhanoi.com.vn, 9am-5pm daily Mon.-Sat., VND420,000-1,245,000) introduces travelers to the finer points of Vietnamese culture through food, language, and walking adventures around the city. Its popular cooking classes take place at the center's charming location on the eastern edge of West Lake, as do a handful of language courses. Several walking tours, along with a much-touted street food tour, take place around the Old and French Quarters. Prices vary depending upon the activity, but all guides are enthusiastic and knowledgeable, making these tours a worthy investment.

Entertainment and Events

NIGHTLIFE

As the sun sets over the capital, Hanoi's nightlife festivities take place in fast-forward, unraveling in a few short hours between sundown and midnight. By 6pm or 7pm, work has barely let out but locals line the streets, gathering on clusters of low, plastic stools to enjoy fresh beer and *do nhau* (drinking food), as they rehash the day's events. An hour later, nightlife is in full swing, with droves of foreigners and Vietnamese packed onto the makeshift furniture of so many independent beer vendors, noshing on grilled meat or snails, a local favorite, washed down with any one of the country's local brews. The streets of the Old Quarter are especially lively, drawing people from all walks of life.

Across town, the well-heeled pay a visit to swanky cocktail lounges and upmarket watering holes around West Lake and throughout the French

Quarter, where top-shelf spirits, terrace seating, and mellow mood music speak to a more refined ambience, while the catch-all bar-and-restaurants near St. Joseph's Cathedral sling cheap beers and other beverages in a casual, laid-back environment. Wherever you are, the night reaches its peak around 9pm, and from there things run on their own steam until midnight, when a fairly strict curfew is enforced and most businesses close their doors for the evening. A handful of bars quietly remain open for another hour or so.

There is hope for late-night revelers. As a city that prides itself on traditional values, Hanoi has been resistant to progress on the nightlife front, but city officials are beginning to come around in the interest of developing tourism. Beyond the weekend street closures around Hoan Kiem Lake, a growing number of bars and clubs are keeping their doors open past midnight.

Bars

True to its name, the **Polite Pub** (5B Bao Khanh, tel. 09/0419-8086, 4pm-midnight daily, VND35,000-150,000) serves as a slightly more upscale watering hole than some of its Old Quarter competition farther north without getting too pretentious. Tucked down a quiet street off Hoan Kiem Lake, the cozy venue serves a list of beer, wine, spirits, and cocktails. Ample seating is available up front, while a pool table occupies the back room.

Lounges

A cozy street-side lounge not far from the Opera House, **Tadioto** (24B Tong Dan, tel. 04/6680-9124, 9am-midnight daily, VND35,000-270,000) exudes a laid-back vibe with plush couches, leather bar stools, and bright red French doors in a prime people-watching neighborhood. Prices are reasonable and a happy hour drink looking out onto Tong Dan is worthwhile. The bar boasts an assortment of beer, wine, and cocktails.

From a rooftop in the French Quarter, Hanoi's chic and sophisticated **Press Club** (59A Ly Thai To, tel. 04/3934-0888, www.hanoi-pressclub.com, 8am-midnight daily, VND100,000-700,000) affords pleasant views of one of the city's most upscale neighborhoods as well as a range of signature cocktails, top-shelf spirits, wine, and beer. Seating is available indoors at the Press Club's elegant bar or outside on a breezy, palm-fringed terrace. Live music acts occasionally pop up here, while regular drink specials, like the Thursday buy-two-get-one-free deal, run throughout the week.

The swanky and sophisticated **88 Lounge** (88 Xuan Dieu, tel. 04/3718-8029, www.88group.vn, 11am-1am Sun.-Wed., 11am-2am Thurs.-Sat., VND50,000-400,000) overlooks West Lake, with three floors of open-air seating that afford top-notch views of the water from an array of antique upholstered chairs. Pair this with dim lighting, a well-stocked downstairs bar, and an impressive collection of fine wines on display, and the place is a hit, functioning as one of the neighborhood's best stand-alone lounges.

Hanoi's Craft Beer Scene

tourists and locals enjoying *bia hoi*

As the workday comes to a close and an army of motorbikes floods the city streets, the place to be in the capital is a small plastic chair by the roadside with an ice-cold glass of *bia hoi* in hand. This light, refreshing lager is a staple of northern nightlife, drawing crowds to the bustling sidewalks of downtown Hanoi on a daily basis. What sets this particular brew apart is its makeup: Local breweries concoct the amber liquid using basic beer ingredients like hops, yeast, and rice. Without any preservatives or additional chemicals, the beer's shelf life becomes especially brief, with most *bia hoi* unfit to drink by the end of the night. Local establishments must plan ahead, ordering just enough to last a single day. In the wee hours of the morning, a representative goes to the brewery to pick up an order of *bia hoi*. From the time it reaches the premises, shopkeepers work to unload as much of their stock as possible, slinging drinks throughout the day, but the rush comes in the evenings, when Hanoi's sidewalks come alive and a healthy drinking culture helps to push sales along. *Bia hoi* is often enjoyed with street-side snacks, known as *do nhau* in Vietnamese. The brew comes in at roughly four percent alcohol by volume, making it a highly drinkable beverage, if a little watery. Best of all, its price tag runs no higher than VND5,000 in the big city, making it far and away the most affordable beverage around. You can also look for the slightly more expensive *bia tuoi*, a similar recipe with a bit more flavor. Both varieties are commonly translated as "fresh beer."

There are many *bia hoi* shops in downtown Hanoi. The most popular is often referred to as **bia hoi corner** (corner of Ta Hien and Luong Ngoc Quyen, 10am-midnight daily). While not all of the corner shops serve genuine *bia hoi*, you'll find plenty of the brew on the southeast edge of the junction. Beyond this swarm of nighttime activity, a clutch of more locally frequented *bia hoi* are situated around Bat Dan and Duong Thanh near the western side of the Old Quarter, though you won't find any English speakers here.

Prices are steep, but these folks know their wines, not to mention everything else, from whiskey and scotch to soju, sake, and tequila.

Clubs

Loud, lively, and filled with nonstop energy, **Dragonfly** (15 Hang Buom, tel. 09/3699-3557, 9pm-1am daily, VND40,000-100,000) is a small Hanoian version of a nightclub, slipped between the shops along Hang Buom. Those looking for a spot to let loose on the dance floor will appreciate the up-tempo beats and cheap drinks. For a slightly quieter atmosphere, head to the second floor, though don't expect to leave here without at least a little hearing damage. If you're looking for a drink earlier in the evening, Dragonfly functions as a café and restaurant during the day; it turns into a nightspot after 9pm.

Live Music

Every evening from 9pm, the loud and lively **Minh's Jazz Club** (1A Trang Tien, tel. 04/3933-6555, www.minhjazzvietnam.com, 8am-4pm daily, live music 9pm-11:30pm daily, VND60,000-200,000) showcases the best of Hanoi's jazz talent. Self-taught saxophonist and accomplished musician Quyen Van Minh, the club's owner, has cultivated an appreciation of jazz in the city, drawing nightly crowds into the intimate café for an impressive live performance. No cover charge is required, though prices double at showtime to accommodate for the musicians.

Bright and eye-catching, the main entrance of **Swing** (21 Trang Tien, tel. 04/3824-5395, www.swinglounge.com.vn, 8am-midnight daily, VND35,000-190,000) is decked out in high-wattage light bulbs, announcing this chic musical venue from a block away. Though it moonlights as an upscale café for the business crowd during the day, the lounge is at its best after dark, when the entire black-and-white space is transformed by nightly performances. The usual beer, wine, and cocktails are on offer, as well as non-alcoholic café beverages, and cozy sofa seating is scattered throughout. Music begins at 9pm and runs until closing time.

Buried down an alley north of West Lake, **Hanoi Rock City** (27/52 To Ngoc Van, tel. 018/8748-7426, www.hanoirockcity.com, 4pm-midnight Sun.-Thurs., 4pm-3am Fri.-Sat., VND50,000-200,000) continues to make its mark on Hanoi's live music scene as one of the premier venues for both local and international artists to showcase their talent. Boasting a spacious interior as well as a sprawling garden area, the funky West Lake venue also hosts the occasional DJ or film screening and keeps a regular list of upcoming acts on its website and Facebook page. Events usually include a cover charge, though they usually cost less than VND100,000.

THE ARTS

Hanoi boasts a glut of Vietnam's most talented artists, from musicians and photographers to lacquer painters, sculptors, and masters of traditional theater and puppetry. Scores of small, independent galleries and cultural centers exist alongside more formal institutions like the national Museum of Fine Arts and the imposing Opera House. Even cafés and a few other small venues have gotten in on the city's arts and culture scene with small film screenings, ongoing exhibitions, artist talks, and other events. For the most up-to-date information, keep an eye on *The Word* (www.wordhanoi.com), with online and print editions that include an events calendar with upcoming shows, concerts, exhibitions, and other performances, as well as **Hanoi Grapevine** (www.hanoigrapevine.com), another reliable event-listing site.

Performing Arts

For everything from ballet to orchestral music, jazz concerts, piano recitals, operas, and traditional Vietnamese theater, Hanoi's historic **Opera House** (1 Trang Tien, tel. 04/3933-0113, www.hanoioperahouse.org.vn, box office 8am-5pm daily) is the go-to venue.

The talented musicians of the **Hanoi Ca Tru Club** (42-44 Hang Bac, tel. 09/7815-6245, www.catru.vn, 8pm daily, VND290,000 Mon.-Sat., VND350,000 Sun.) put on daily performances in the heart of the Old Quarter. In a small, intimate space, the hourlong show celebrates *ca tru,* a centuries-old form of northern Vietnamese poetry set to music, typically featuring one female singer, a male instrumentalist, and a drummer. While the traditional music is well-known throughout the Red River Delta area, *ca tru* is something of a dying art, as most of its musicians are older. Today, accomplished musicians keep the tradition alive through regular shows, usually for foreign visitors. The audience is small, and participation by audience members is often required. Tickets can be purchased throughout the week (8am-5pm); aim for one day in advance. It's sometimes possible to snag a seat on the evening of a performance. If you can't finagle a seat with the Hanoi Ca Tru Club, you can also try the **Thang Long Ca Tru Club** (28 Hang Buom, tel. 012/2326-6897, www.catruthanglong.com, 8pm Thurs. and Sat., VND270,000), another well-known local troupe.

The vivacious characters of **Thang Long Water Puppet Theater** (57B Dinh Tien Hoang, tel. 04/3824-9494, www.thanglongwaterpuppet.org, shows 3pm-8pm daily, box office 8:30am-8:30pm daily, VND100,000) know how to make a splash, zipping across their watery stage several times a day at Hanoi's best-known *mua roi nuoc* (water puppet) venue. As early as the 11th century, rice paddies and other shallow waters in the Red River Delta served as performance spaces for these lacquered wooden puppets and their masters, who maneuver the characters from behind a bamboo screen. Nowadays, the performances, combined with lively voice actors and traditional Vietnamese music, are a popular cultural attraction for visitors to the city. Each show runs around 50 minutes, featuring a handful of individual vignettes. While the performance takes place in Vietnamese, the watery antics of these puppets provide enough information that no translation is necessary.

Galleries and Museums

Spread over three floors, exhibits at the **Museum of Fine Arts** (66 Nguyen Thai Hoc, tel. 04/3823-3084, www.vnfam.vn, 8:30am-5pm daily, VND40,000) cover the creative achievements of Vietnamese painters, sculptors, and other craftspeople from the 11th century onward. Beginning with the stone and wood carvings of several of Vietnam's early dynasties, displays proceed chronologically through the country's artistic development, showcasing beautiful functional pieces and religious relics from the earliest days of the empire before carrying on to the 19th- and 20th-century fusion of Western ideas and materials with Vietnamese aesthetics. The resulting artwork, which includes vivid lacquer paintings alongside other mediums, like oil and acrylic, remains straightforward, depicting everyday Vietnamese scenes, portraits, and still life renderings. The most recent paintings hail from the 1980s and '90s. Its sole showroom of conceptual art is a letdown. The museum overall is a rewarding stop on your tour of the city and remains intriguing for both its artwork and the visible evolution of ideas over the years. Visitors are free to explore the many rooms of this 1930s colonial building on their own; a handy map is provided upon arrival that helps guide you through the museum's many numbered exhibits.

One part art space, one part café, the hip and happening **Manzi** (14 Phan Huy Ich, tel. 04/3716-3397, 8am-10:30pm daily) sits a few blocks beyond the Old Quarter and hosts regular art exhibitions, talks, film screenings, and music and dance performances within its updated French colonial digs. White walls and minimal furniture give the place a gallery feel. Visitors are invited to sit and enjoy the café, either downstairs amid the calm of alley life or upstairs with the art. Both international and Vietnamese artists have been featured in Manzi's two-story space, and its rotating schedule of cultural performances and events is updated regularly on Facebook.

Located just behind the Temple of Literature and a short walk from the Museum of Fine Arts, Hanoi's **Goethe Institute** (56-58 Nguyen Thai Hoc, tel. 04/3734-2251, www.goethe.de, 8:30am-noon and 1pm-5:30pm Mon.-Fri.) remains an active part of the local art scene, holding regular exhibits, workshops, and film screenings in its **DOCLAB.** Many of these events are free and open to the public. Check out the institute's website or Facebook page for a list of upcoming exhibitions.

The pristine white walls of **Green Palm Gallery** (15 Trang Tien, tel. 04/3936-4757, www.greenpalmgallery.com, 8am-8pm daily) display some of Hanoi's top contemporary talents, such as Nguyen Thanh Binh, Nguyen The Dung, and Nguyen Manh Hung. With a layout that pays homage to traditional Vietnamese architecture, paintings and sculptures are spread out over three rooms, separated at the center by a small courtyard. Each piece is given its due space, and knowledgeable employees are on hand to answer questions. The gallery also has a second location (39 Hang Gai, tel. 09/1321-8496, 8am-8pm daily) closer to downtown, but the Trang Tien branch offers more peace and quiet.

With a laundry list of featured artists, the **Apricot Gallery** (40B Hang Bong, tel. 04/3828-8965, www.apricotgallery.com.vn, 8am-8pm daily) is one of Hanoi's most established showrooms, bringing together a variety of materials and aesthetic styles under one roof. Paintings tend to be oil or acrylic, though there are a few lacquer works here, too, and the long, narrow exhibit space, which extends a few floors up above, offers plenty to admire as you wander from room to room.

FESTIVALS AND EVENTS

While the **Mid-Autumn Festival** (early-mid Sept.) sweeps across the whole country, Hanoi's festivities are especially lively. The holiday, which falls on the 15th day of the eighth lunar month, typically takes place during the first half of September and features scores of colorful decorations. Brightly hued paper lanterns hang from every shop and house in the city, many of them originating from **Hang Ma,** which becomes the city's very own *pho long den* (lantern street) in the weeks leading up to the celebration. Running the gamut from traditional red-and-yellow lanterns to cartoon-shaped paper torches, shops along this narrow Old Quarter road do big business for the holiday, as local families, many of them with young children, partake in the festivities with paper lanterns and moon cake *(banh trung thu),* a round, dense pastry with a reputation not unlike fruitcake: pretty, ornamental, and not nearly as delicious as it looks.

Shopping

Hanoi's compact and chaotic Old Quarter is a microcosm of dressmakers and tailors, craftspeople, carpenters, souvenir vendors, and galleries. One-stop convenience may elude the city's busy streets, but avid shoppers will appreciate the Hanoian retail experience, stumbling upon small, charming boutiques and modest, out-of-the-way shops, each bringing its own unique personality to the multifaceted neighborhood. Independent designers and skilled artisans display their finest wares, often at a price, while mass-produced items like T-shirts, buttons, and hats fill the narrow crevices between buildings, allowing travelers of all budgets to partake in Hanoi's commercial streets. While most of the city's downtown businesses use price tags, the cost of common souvenirs is negotiable wherever you are.

the enormous Dong Xuan Market

Dong Xuan Market

The sprawling **Dong Xuan Market** (Dong Xuan and Cau Dong, tel. 04/3825-7832, 6am-6pm daily), just west of Long Bien Bridge, packs everything under the sun into its two-story shelter. The French-built trading center is a Hanoian institution, famous for its array of products and so popular that it has spilled out onto the streets, turning the road in front of the building into a lively shopping area that becomes the city's night market after dark. Expect to find cheap souvenirs, along with countless bolts of fabric, T-shirts, and many other items.

Hom Market

For fabric shopping, **Hom Market** (Pho Hue, sunrise-sunset daily) just south of Hoan Kiem Lake is the go-to venue, lined with stall upon stall of materials at bargain prices. The usual market items are sold here, from

SHOPPING

The Clothes Make the Traveler

Though much of Hanoi is a retail paradise for women's clothing, it can be hard to know where to start your shopping adventure. The Old Quarter, particularly around Hang Gai and Hang Bong, is chock-full of high-quality brands like **Tan My Design** (61 Hang Gai, tel. 04/3825-1579, www.tanmydesign. com, 8:30am-7pm daily) and **Ha Dong Silk** (102 Hang Gai, tel. 04/3928-5056, hadongsilks@gmail.com, 8am-8pm daily). A handful of standouts in the Cathedral District are worth a visit, such as **Marie-linh** (74 Hang Trong, tel. 04/3928-6304, www.marie-linh.com, 9am-6pm daily) and **Chula** (18 Nha Chung, tel. 09/0425-8960, www.chulafashion.com, 9am-9pm daily). Much of the clothing on offer is made with Vietnamese sizes in mind. Those who are larger than the average Vietnamese woman may want to check out shops like **Things of Substance** (5 Nha Tho, tel. 04/3828-6965, www.thingsof-substance.com, 9am-9pm daily) or the tailors in the Old Quarter or West Lake.

For budget shoppers, the long road (known as Hang Dao, Hang Ngang, or Hang Duong at different points) leading from Hoan Kiem Lake to Dong Xuan Market holds a host of clothing and souvenir shops, as does the intersection where Hang Dao and Hang Gai connect. Shops like **Ginkgo** (79 Hang Gai, tel. 04/3938-2265, www.ginkgo-vietnam.com, 8am-10pm daily) and **Orange** (36 Luong Ngoc Quyen, tel. 04/3935-1387, 9am-10pm daily) offer affordable T-shirts and bags, while **Tagilis** (12 Hang Bong, tel. 09/3440-2974, www.tagilis.wordpress.com, 9am-9pm daily) is an affordable tailor option. Retail outfits along the Old Quarter's Ma May and Ngo Huyen in the Cathedral District also carry the standard array of souvenirs, T-shirts, casual pants, and sundresses.

The options for men's clothing are fewer and limited to standard shirts and shorts. Keep an eye out for the minimal offerings in local boutiques. The streets south of Hoan Kiem Lake toward Hom Market hold a handful of more exciting men's options, as does **Zed's Threads** (36 To Ngoc Van, tel. 04/6258-0208, www.zedsthreads.com, 8:30am-5:30pm Mon.-Sat.) in West Lake, though none of these are unique to Vietnam, but are instead a more affordable version of what you might find at home.

food and household products to shoes, clothing, and other goods, but the real reason to venture into its maze of vendors is the innumerable bolts of fabric. Be sure to haggle, as Hom Market's shrewd businesswomen can drive a hard bargain.

Night Market

Hanoi's regular **night market** (Hang Dao north to Dong Xuan Market, 7pm-midnight Fri.-Sun.) runs from the end of Hang Dao north all the way to Dong Xuan Market, turning the road into a pedestrian-only affair flush with shops selling clothing, dry goods, and souvenirs. Be sure to haggle on this road, as prices tend to start high. Purchasing multiple items can usually get you a discount. While the bazaar only takes place on weekends, many vendors still set up smaller versions of their street stalls on the other days of the week.

SHOPPING DISTRICTS
Trang Tien

Wedged between the southern end of Hoan Kiem Lake and the Red River a few blocks to the east, Trang Tien is Hanoi's luxury shopping neighborhood, replete with high-end fashion, international brands, and familiar designer labels. Ply the narrow streets that spider off August Revolution Square, and you'll discover droves of art galleries, swanky boutiques, and posh cafés.

Running the length of a city block, **Trang Tien Plaza** (corner of Dinh Tien Hoang and Trang Tien, tel. 04/3937-8599, www.trangtienplaza.vn, 9:30am-9:30pm Mon.-Fri., 9am-10pm Sat.-Sun.) houses several international luxury brands, including Bulgari, Cartier, and Lancome, along with designer labels such as Louis Vuitton, Dior, and Versace, over six floors. The center was first built in 1901 to accommodate the city's French colonial

Trang Tien Plaza

The Streets of the Old Quarter

In centuries past, each narrow road in the Old Quarter carried a specific product. Hang Quat, for instance, sold fans, or *quat*, while Hang Giay made its money from paper, or *giay*. Cha Ca was where you went to buy grilled fish, silver was on Hang Bac, and Hang Duong held much of the city's sugar supply. Today, many of these streets have changed trades, but the traditional names have stuck. Hang Dau, the former oil street, now specializes in shoes, for instance.

shoppers. Its current incarnation opened to the public in 2013 as Hanoi's first luxury shopping center.

The **Foreign Language Bookstore** (64 Trang Tien, tel. 04/3825-7376, 8am-9pm daily), just down the road from Trang Tien Plaza, stocks recent American and European magazines such as *Time, Elle, The Economist,* and *Marie Claire,* along with the usual government-approved collection of English-language classics. The shop's section of Vietnam-related books up front gives way to a cache of souvenir items and road and city maps.

Old Quarter

Squeezed into an impossibly small neighborhood north of the lake, Hanoi's historic Old Quarter offers some of the best and most diverse shopping in the city, with stores to fit every budget and taste. From sleek, well-crafted furniture to eye-catching independent boutiques, traditional handicrafts, dime-a-dozen souvenirs, and the odd art gallery, **Hang Gai** and its nearby lanes represent the bulk of the area's offerings. There is also the occasional shop slipped between restaurants and hotels around Ma May, as well as a few of the more affordable souvenir shops buried within the backpacker alley off Ly Quoc Su near the cathedral. Head down sleepy Au Trieu on either side of St. Joseph's, and the hip clothing stores and independent labels reappear.

For fun, colorful, Vietnam-inspired T-shirts, both **Orange** (36 Luong Ngoc Quyen, tel. 04/3935-1387, 9am-10pm daily) and **Ginkgo** (79 Hang Gai, tel. 04/3938-2265, www.ginkgo-vietnam.com, 8am-10pm daily) offer well-made, affordable men's and women's threads with more originality than the stock souvenir items around town. Ginkgo also has a second location (44 Hang Be, tel. 04/3926-4769, 8am-10pm daily) removed from the frenzy of Hang Gai.

Pairing the roaring 1920s with vibrant, edgy prints and colors, **Magonn** (76 Ba Trieu, tel. 04/3633-0036, www.magonn.com.vn, 9am-10pm daily) brings an old-world class to its chic, modern style. The well-stocked hipster boutique features a line of original women's clothing created by a young, Hanoi-based design duo, running the gamut from classy to casual with sleek pencil skirts, flirty A-line frocks, and drop-waist dresses.

The smart, understated clothing at **Indigo Store** (33 Van Mieu, tel.

04/3719-3090, 8am-7pm daily) may not jump out at you, but the beauty of these items lies in their simplicity. Using traditional methods, the shop sticks to indigo-dyed clothing for both men and women, using all-natural fabrics and embroidery courtesy of Vietnam's ethnic minorities, whose colorful, intricate needlework jumps out from the plain blue background.

One of a few skilled tailors on the block, **Ha Dong Silk** (102 Hang Gai, tel. 04/3928-5056, hadongsilks@gmail.com, 8am-8pm daily) fashions high-quality custom items. The shop also boasts a range of ready-made women's clothing along with accessories and jewelry. The ground floor of the building houses off-the-rack options; the fabric selection is upstairs.

The two floors of local favorite **Tan My Design** (61 Hang Gai, tel. 04/3825-1579, www.tanmydesign.com, 8:30am-7pm daily) are a catchall of jewelry, accessories, women's clothing, and housewares, run by three generations of a Hanoian family. From dresses to necklaces, bags, and bedding, Tan My pairs bright, bold colors with a distinctly Vietnamese flair, drawing upon the best of the old and the new. There is a small black-and-white café in the back of the narrow, all-white store. Across the street is Tan My's original location (66 Hang Gai, tel. 04/3825-1579, www.tanmy-embroidery.com.vn, 8am-8pm daily), which specializes in beautiful hand-embroidered silks and other fabrics.

Perhaps the most affordable tailor on the block, **Tagilis** (12 Hang Bong, tel. 09/3440-2974, www.tagilis.wordpress.com, 9am-9pm daily) specializes in well-made women's dresses in a range of materials and styles. The cheerful folks who run the shop are willing to copy designs or come up with new ones, and the average knee-length dress should set you back around VND670,000, give or take a few dollars depending upon the cut and fabric. Ready-made items are also available in bright colors and prints.

A long, narrow shop above the beautiful silk women's clothing of **Ha Linh Thu** (87 Hang Gai, tel. 04/3828-6758, www.halinhthu.vn, 9am-9pm daily), **Van Loi** (87 Hang Gai, tel. 04/3828-6758, www.vanloi.com, 9am-9pm daily) does a trade in beautiful wooden furniture, mother-of-pearl dishware, lacquer trays, and other home furnishings. Colorful or traditional, ostentatious or reserved, all items are produced locally and with care. The shop's smaller kitchen items and decorative pieces make easy-to-pack souvenirs.

Cathedral District

A less hectic extension of the Old Quarter, Hanoi's Cathedral District is home to a handful of unique, creative boutiques selling women's clothing, ceramics, and other knickknacks. Prices are a little more reasonable here, away from the main shopping drag. This area is still well within the bounds of Hanoi's more touristy area, so expect to find plenty of foreign shoppers and souvenirs here.

Hidden amid a street full of European restaurants and dwarfed by the nearby St. Joseph's Cathedral, Japanese brand **Nagu** (20 Nha Tho, tel. 04/3928-8020, www.zantoc.com, 8:30am-8pm daily) offers a combination of simple, understated women's clothing, accessories, homewares, and kids' toys with a local touch.

The vision of a French-Vietnamese designer, **Marie-linh** (74 Hang Trong, tel. 04/3928-6304, www.marie-linh.com, 9am-6pm daily) creates smart and affordable women's clothing. Combining high-quality fabrics with Eastern and Western influences, the shop's shirts, pants, shorts, and dresses offer casual comfort without sacrificing style. A more upscale version of Marie-linh is open a few doors down, as is another location (11 Nha Tho, tel. 04/3928-8773, www.marie-linh.com, 9am-6pm daily) nearby.

A color-coded boutique that boasts "Western sizes at Vietnamese prices," **Things of Substance** (5 Nha Tho, tel. 04/3828-6965, www.thingsofsubstance.com, 9am-9pm daily) features women's wear with vibrant tops and flowing cotton and jersey dresses. There are few fitted items here, but the flowy styles are ideal for traveling and work well in the heat. Western-sized pants and a range of funky jewelry round out the shop's offerings.

In the wide, shallow storefront at **Marena Hanoi** (28 Nha Chung, tel. 04/3828-5542, 9am-7pm daily) there is barely enough room to turn around. Its shelves are packed with elegant, well-made ceramics and lacquerware, with much of its stock sticking to traditional themes. Simple blue-and-white designs adorn plates, tea sets, mugs, and small bowls, while lacquer trays and boxes boast brilliant reds or blacks. All items are handmade and prices are reasonable.

Packed with plush quilts and bright home furnishings, **Mekong Creations** (58 Hang Trong, tel. 04/3824-4607, www.mekong-plus.com, 9am-9pm daily) offers well-made products for a good cause. Aimed at providing women in southern Vietnam and Cambodia with a sustainable income, this nonprofit organization has been assisting local communities since 2001. An array of quilts, bamboo products, and other housewares feature in this tiny shop, with half of the proceeds from each sale going back to the village from which the product came. For more variety, swing by **Mekong Quilts** (13 Hang Bac, tel. 04/3926-4831, www.mekong-plus.com, 9am-9pm daily) nearby.

Ba Dinh District

Though this district is reserved more for historical sights than retail outlets, the one or two shops you'll find in Ba Dinh District are well worth your time.

54 Traditions (30 Hang Bun, tel. 04/3715-1569, www.54traditions.vn, 8:30am-6pm daily) celebrates the diverse cultures of Vietnam's 54 ethnicities, particularly its northern minority groups. Founded in 2004, the shop not only sells ancient artifacts, shamanic artwork, textiles, jewelry, and everyday objects of minority people, but also educates its customers on these items. Each purchase comes with at least 1,000 words of information on the object. Some stock dates all the way back to the Dong Son culture, and many items are museum-grade quality. Items range from a few dollars to a few thousand dollars.

Tailor Made

Along Hang Gai and throughout the Old Quarter, tailors are easy to come by but quality and affordability together can be hard to find. A handful of standouts offer reliable service and skill at reasonable prices. Those who wish to have any tailoring done in Hanoi should plan ahead, as tailors in the capital tend to require more time than the speedy seamstresses of Hoi An. The average purchase can take anywhere from a few days to a week to complete, not including extra fittings or alterations. Most Hanoian tailors stock their own fabrics, saving you the trouble of visiting the market, though be prepared to pay a premium for this service. Whether you opt for the materials in-store or choose to purchase your own, it's best to swing by your preferred shop ahead of time to ensure that you buy enough of the required fabric and to get an idea of how much you should be paying for it.

Tagilis (12 Hang Bong, tel. 09/3440-2974, www.tagilis.wordpress.com, 9am-9pm daily) in the Old Quarter is your best bet for reasonably priced women's clothing. For a bit more quality try **Ha Dong Silk** (102 Hang Gai, tel. 04/3928-5056, hadongsilks@gmail.com, 8am-8pm daily), located on the same Old Quarter street, which provides a more upmarket range of fabrics and services. If it's more sophisticated tailoring you seek, West Lake shops like **Clom's Closet** (31A Xuan Dieu, tel. 04/3718-8233, clomscloset.com, 10am-8pm daily) and the high-fashion **Chula** (43 Nhat Chieu, tel. 09/0425-8960, www.chulafashion.com, 9am-6pm daily) come at a price, but their quality is unmatched. Men looking for affordable, well-made dress shirts and pants would do well to check out **Zed's Threads** (36 To Ngoc Van, tel. 04/6258-0208, www.zedsthreads.com, 8:30am-5:30pm Mon.-Sat.), a men's-only tailoring shop also located in West Lake.

Avid readers will be at home among the stacks of **Bookworm** (44 Chau Long, tel. 04/3715-3711, www.bookwormhanoi.com, 9am-7pm daily), an independent English-language bookstore. The shop boasts over 15,000 new and used titles in its two-story collection. A smaller room dedicated to Southeast Asia and Vietnam touches on topics such as history, culture, and local issues.

West Lake

For a calmer shopping experience, the West Lake neighborhood is home to more upmarket shopping, falling somewhere in between the Old Quarter and Trang Tien. Though it's less accessible than its southern counterparts, with shops fewer and farther between, the neighborhood includes a unique set of tailors for both men and women, not to mention a greater chance of finding Western sizes than Hanoi's downtown shops.

Full of vivid colors and daring designs, the handmade dresses at **Chula** (43 Nhat Chieu, tel. 09/0425-8960, www.chulafashion.com, 9am-6pm daily) are sure to get you noticed. The brainchild of a Spanish duo, this independent design house specializes in formal wear, creating vibrant, original pieces and tailor-made items for women. A wide array of ready-made outfits are available for purchase. You can also commission the skilled Diego to fashion something custom. Prices are similar to American department stores, but the quality is unparalleled. You can also find Chula's dresses, skirts, jackets and tops at a second location (18 Nha Chung, tel. 09/0425-8960, www.chulafashion.com, 9am-9pm daily) near the cathedral downtown.

Stepping into **Clom's Closet** (31A Xuan Dieu, tel. 04/3718-8233, clomscloset.com, 10am-8pm daily) feels like entering a very fashionable wardrobe. Tastefully decorated and featuring men's and women's clothing, handbags, and accessories, this upmarket tailor produces truly beautiful formal wear using high-quality materials from around the world. Western prices apply here, but the quality and skill of Clom's tailors is well worth the cost.

While its fashion may not be as bold as other shops, **Zed's Threads** (36 To Ngoc Van, tel. 04/6258-0208, www.zedsthreads.com, 8:30am-5:30pm Mon.-Sat.) is one of the only menswear stores in Hanoi that offers strictly men's clothing in sizes that fit Westerners. A range of quality shirts, pants, and suits take up the shop's racks. Made-to-measure services (8am-noon and 1pm-5pm Mon.-Sat.) are available, free of charge, though you'll have to make an appointment beforehand, either by phone or online.

Sports and Recreation

There are a few activities for recreation once you've exhausted your sightseeing and shopping options. You'll find charming green spaces around the city. Spas are a growing industry, as are cooking classes, for those keen to master the art of Vietnamese cuisine.

PARKS

Scattered throughout Ba Dinh, Hoan Kiem, and Hai Ba Trung districts are Hanoi's array of small but well-loved parks, which serve as exercise tracks for early-risers, meeting spots for midday revelers, and communal areas for friends and family once the workday adjourns. While few of these green spaces could rival the parks you might find at home in terms of size, Hanoi's dozens of miniature clearings are a pleasant break from the madness of its usual hustle and bustle. The ring around **Hoan Kiem Lake** is the most popular of these areas, drawing hundreds of locals and tourists each day, including a small but devoted collection of young Vietnamese students hoping to strike up a conversation with a passing foreigner to practice their English.

Opposite Hoan Kiem Lake sits **Ly Thai To Park** (Dinh Tien Hoang between Le Lai and Le Thach), a modest square dominated by its imposing statue of the emperor of the same name. As the founder of Thang Long (what's now known as Hanoi), Ly Thai To features heavily on street signs, businesses, and monuments throughout Hanoi. The open concrete square is packed with early-morning exercisers or rollerblading school kids later in the day.

A small wedge of green opposite the Military History Museum, **Lenin Park** (Dien Bien Phu between Hoang Dieu and Nguyen Tri Phuong) bears a domineering stone statue of its namesake at the far end of the clearing overlooking the city's famous Flag Tower. Trees line the edge of the concrete space, acting as a buffer between the downtown traffic and the relative peace of the square.

For a genuine escape from the Old Quarter chaos, Hanoi's **Botanical Garden** (Vuon Bach Thao, Hoang Hoa Tham, 7am-10pm daily, VND2,000) offers some much-appreciated silence in a city where noise pollution can wear on a person. In truth, this peaceful green space is pretty average, but thanks to its location and size, the pleasant grounds, equipped with two fish ponds, plenty of seating, and a collection of blocky, abstract sculptures, take the edge off Hanoi's frantic traffic. Animal-lovers would do well to bypass the cage near the entrance, as the birds inside are not particularly well looked after. While the park is a lovely place during the day, it's wise to stay away after dark, as this is a frequent hangout for some of Hanoi's more unsavory characters.

AMUSEMENT PARKS

One of Vincom's two mega malls, **Royal City** (72A Nguyen Trai, tel. 04/6276-7799, www.vincom.com.vn, 9:30am-10pm daily) goes above and beyond your average retail center with an indoor waterfall, movie theater, bowling alley, arcade, water park, and an ice skating rink. Entry to the mall is free of charge, but use of the facilities costs money (VND50,000-200,000).

Lenin Park provides a relaxing place to read the paper.

CYCLING

On the bicycle front, Hanoi has come a long way in recent years, cultivating a healthy crop of both local and expat cyclists who have taken to its streets in style, pedaling everything from flashy fixies to sleek, ultra-light road bikes to vintage, basket-toting city vehicles. Several small cycling communities exist throughout the city, meeting up for a jaunt down one of the larger roads or around West Lake. The capital has encountered some growing pains recently, as it attempts to make Hanoi a more bicycle-friendly city without altering the breakneck, chaotic traffic that congests its downtown streets. Bicycle rentals are possible and guided tours can be found through the city's best-known foreign cycling community, The Hanoi Bicycle Collective.

For cycling enthusiasts, a visit to **The Hanoi Bicycle Collective** (33 Nhat Chieu, tel. 04/3718-3156, www.thbc.vn, 9am-7pm Mon.-Sat.) is a must. Founded in 2009 by Spaniard Guim Valls Tereul and his Vietnamese wife Thuy Anh Nguyen, the shop has served as a base for Hanoi's foreign cycling community, offering bicycles and cycling gear for sale, city tours for curious travelers, and a regular "bike doctor" (Mon.-Sat.) to assist with repairs. The shop offers a complimentary maintenance check to those cycling through Hanoi on a longer trip. The shop also runs regular cycling tours (VND860,000-950,000) of downtown Hanoi and the West Lake area.

SWIMMING

Summertime temperatures in the city can be unforgiving, and one of the better ways to beat the heat is with a trip to the pool. A handful of high-end hotels allow pool access to non-guests, but day passes verge on exorbitant. The venues in this section are a more attractive option for those on a budget.

Overlooking scenic West Lake, the pool at **Thang Loi Resort** (200 Yen Phu, tel. 04/3829-4211 ext. 374, www.thangloihotel.vn, 6am-6pm daily, VND80,000) stays open year-round and offers changing rooms, lounge chairs, and access to the resort's restaurant and bar services. Though the pool is small, its location makes for a pleasant escape from the city's noise and affords nice views of the surrounding area. Bring your own towel, as these are not provided. The place gets crowded on weekends, usually in the afternoons, as local families bring their children for a swim.

Hanoi's only saltwater swimming venue, the **Army Guesthouse Pool** (33C Pham Ngu Lao, tel. 04/3825-2896, armyhotel@fpt.vn, 6:30am-9pm daily, VND90,000) escapes much of the downtown chaos, hiding at the end of a quiet, tree-lined avenue behind the Opera House. The lanes are large, and plenty of free space affords serious swimmers the opportunity to get some laps in. This spot is best avoided on weekends, namely in the afternoons, as families often turn up for downtime at the pool.

MASSAGES AND SPAS

While Hanoi boasts its fair share of quality massage parlors, spa services in the capital are more expensive than other destinations in the country. Tipping 15-20 percent is a standard practice in most massage parlors.

Aimed at training disadvantaged local youth for a career in massage therapy, **Just Massage** (237 Au Co, tel. 04/2123-6655, www.justmassage. org.vn, 9am-9pm daily, VND250,000-500,000) offers everything from Swedish and shiatsu massages to hot stones and aromatherapy treatments. Staff are friendly and speak English, allowing you to communicate with your massage therapist, and prices won't break the bank.

The tranquil **SF Spa** (30 Cua Dong, tel. 04/3747-5301, www.sfintercare. com, 9am-11pm daily, VND280,000-1,200,000), located on the western edge of the Old Quarter, is among Hanoi's more ambient retreats. Featuring a variety of foot and full-body massages, body treatments, facials, waxing, and all-encompassing spa packages, this charming day spa boasts a chic, simple modern decor along with experienced, English-speaking massage therapists. The last booking of the day is at 9:30pm.

Located within the Elegance Diamond Hotel on the eastern edge of the Old Quarter is **La Siesta Spa** (32 Lo Su, tel. 04/3935-1632, www.elegance-hospitality.com, 9am-9pm daily, VND380,000-1,250,000). Boasting the same range of high-quality spa services, massages, facials, and body scrubs, the company's downtown facility provides a tranquil escape from the chaos outdoors, as well as several package treatments inspired by the principle of the five elements: earth, water, fire, metal, and wood. There is also a second location (94 Ma May, tel. 04/3926-3642) in the Old Quarter, which has the same hours.

COOKING CLASSES

Right in the heart of the Old Quarter, the **Blue Butterfly** (61 Hang Buom, tel. 04/3926-3845, www.bluebutterflyrestaurant.com, 9am and 3:30pm daily, VND1,225,000) runs half-day cooking classes every morning and afternoon. Three-hour courses begin with a trip to Dong Xuan Market, where a local chef will explain the finer points of Vietnamese produce before participants head back to the restaurant, don a chef's hat and apron, and begin to cook. Three basic but delicious local dishes feature on the class menu, all of which are included in the recipe book presented at the end of the session. Classes are small with up to 10 or 12 per group. This is a fun and different way for novice chefs to learn about local culture.

Boasting a range of courses designed by Australian chef Tracey Lister, co-author of three books on Vietnamese cuisine, the **Hanoi Cooking Center** (44 Chau Long, tel. 04/3715-0088, www.hanoicookingcentre. com, 8:30am-5:30pm daily, VND1,320,000) may offer the most expensive cooking classes in the city, but its experienced staff provide a clean environment, top-of-the-line cookware, and plenty of hands-on instruction about Vietnamese cuisine. Choose from several themed courses, including a vegan tofu option, a session on barbecue and salads, and a half-day class devoted to spring rolls. Each course runs around four hours, with three in the kitchen and one to enjoy your sumptuous creations, and class sizes average 8-10 people. The center also offers street eats and market tours (Mon.-Sat., VND1,320,000), which take visitors on a four-hour trip around town, enjoying several varieties of local fare. Their children's cooking classes (VND1,320,000) allow young chefs to partake in some basic, supervised cooking. Hanoi Cooking Center runs a small café (9am-5:30pm daily, VND20,000-140,000) on the ground floor, serving mostly Western meals as well as European and Vietnamese coffee.

Food

Holding the distinction of best pho in Vietnam, the capital city collectively enjoys thousands of helpings each morning. Other Hanoian specialties earn equal notoriety for their flavors and textures. The unsung hero—made famous by Barack Obama and Anthony Bourdain—is *bun cha,* a delicious northern version of grilled meat and rice noodles doused in *nuoc cham,* a diluted fish sauce that comes with pickled veggies, fresh greens, and the occasional fried spring roll. You'll find this mouthwatering specialty on every street corner and likely smell it from a few blocks away, as the scent of barbecue floats up from street stalls. What Hanoi does, it does well: Mouthwatering, square-shaped seafood spring rolls, also known as *nem cua be,* are a must-eat in the capital. Several *cha ca* (pan-fried fish) restaurants round out the best Vietnamese offerings.

Hanoi's non-Vietnamese fare offers plenty of variety, from Indian and Malaysian meals to Thai, French, and American. Upscale eateries make a greater effort in the service department, opting for a Western approach, and there are more than a few foreign chefs and owners behind some of the city's well-known Western restaurants. The need for reservations is greater here, as the limited space of the Old Quarter means that dining rooms fill up fast.

The streets of Hanoi are a good place to experience roadside dining in Vietnam. Crammed onto already-busy sidewalks and hidden down narrow alleys, chefs serve everything from tasty Vietnamese sandwiches to piping hot soups, rice porridge, barbecue, and local specialties, often at VND40,000 or less per meal.

Safe street food is easy to find, provided you stick to clean outdoor kitchens. When in doubt, look for hot meals, such as soups or grilled meats. High temperatures tend to eliminate some of the risk.

OLD QUARTER
Cafés and Bakeries
Modest and unassuming, **Giang Cafe** (39 Nguyen Huu Huan, tel. 09/8989-2298, www.cafegiang.vn, 7am-10pm daily, VND15,000-30,000), in business since 1946, is hidden from the street by a narrow passageway between two larger storefronts. Try a cup of Hanoi's famous *ca phe trung* (a combination

of egg yolks, condensed milk, and Vietnamese coffee). This may not sound appetizing, but the thick, decadent concoction is a treat on a cold day. The modest shop serves regular coffee, tea, and other refreshments at local prices. Its founder, Nguyen Giang, worked as a bartender at the legendary Metropole hotel before opening Giang Cafe.

French-Vietnamese Fusion

One of Hanoi's best-known venues, **Green Tangerine** (48 Hang Be, tel. 04/3825-1286, www.greentangerinehanoi.com, 10am-11pm daily, VND175,000-600,000) specializes in French and Vietnamese fusion, pairing unlikely ingredients to create unique and memorable dishes. The restaurant's 1928 colonial villa makes a worthy setting for a fancy meal. Prices run high, but the set menus offer decent value, with two-course lunches beginning at VND265,000. Given its popularity (it has been featured in a handful of high-profile publications, as well as on CNN's Travel website), reservations are a good idea.

Gastropubs

A classy pub and grill, **The Moose & Roo** (42B Ma May, tel. 04/3266-8081, www.mooseandroo.com, 11am-midnight Mon.-Fri., 10am-midnight Sat., 10am-11pm Sun., VND125,000-300,000) serves hearty pub dishes, from burgers, steaks, and savory pies to full Western breakfasts. Beer, wine, and cocktails are on offer, including hard-to-find top-shelf scotches and whiskeys. Dining in this cozy narrow space is well worth the price, and it makes for an excellent spot to unwind after a day of shopping and sightseeing.

Indian

The best of Hanoi's clutch of Indian restaurants, **Little India** (32 Hang Tre, tel. 04/3926-1859, www.littleindiahanoi.com, 10:30am-2:30pm and 6pm-10:30pm daily, VND50,000-200,000) boasts not only an impressive range of Indian cuisine but also a list of Malaysian dishes, including *nasi goreng* and beef *rendang,* as well as a few Chinese meals. Portions are generous, prices are right, and the staff aim to please. As a 100-percent halal establishment, you won't find alcohol here, but you're no more than a few blocks from nightlife venues, should you require a nightcap afterward.

Street Food

A Hanoi institution, ★ **Xoi Yen** (35B Nguyen Huu Huan, tel. 04/3934-1950, 6am-midnight daily, VND15,000-50,000) is always packed with locals. Specializing in savory *xoi* (sticky rice), this restaurant features a menu of assorted toppings, including meats such as *xa xiu,* also known as *char siu* (Chinese-style roast pork), chicken, *cha* (a type of Vietnamese processed meat), or claypot-braised pork, which accompany your choice of sticky rice. Low tables and stools populate both the ground floor and the open-air second story. Visit the one on the corner and not its impostor next door.

Directly opposite Hang Da Market is a small, open-front shop that doles out tasty *mien luon* (87 Hang Dieu, tel. 04/3826-7943, 7am-10:30pm daily, VND20,000-50,000). The bowls of piping hot soup feature glass noodles and fried eel. Order the rice porridge or any of the other eel dishes from a large picture menu mounted on the wall. The metal-and-plastic furniture fit right in with the street-food vibe.

Fresh, flavorful, and good enough for seconds, the *bun bo nam bo* (67 Hang Dieu, 7am-10pm daily, VND60,000) at the skinny storefront near Hang Da Market is a popular choice among locals. Metal tables line the long, narrow dining area and a dexterous assembly line prepares heaping portions of the tasty rice noodle and beef dish, complete with fresh greens, pickled carrots, peanuts, and sauce.

While there are hundreds of street stalls serving this classic Hanoian dish, the ★ *bun cha* (34 Hang Than, tel. 04/3927-0879, 9am-2pm or until sold out daily, VND35,000) on Hang Than is the best of its kind. Hearty helpings of grilled pork and ground meat come swimming in *nuoc cham*, a lighter cousin of fish sauce, accompanied by pickled carrots and daikon. Add rice noodles and as many fresh greens as you'd like, stir, and enjoy. This spot only opens for lunch, and its product is well known among locals. If you're short on time or prefer to stay closer to the Old Quarter, **Bun Cha Dac Kim** (1 Hang Manh, tel. 04/3828-5022, www.bunchahangmanh.vn, 8am-10pm daily, VND60,000) is another well-known local spot for *bun cha*. The owners overcharge foreigners, sometimes as much as VND90,000 for a meal.

Vietnamese

Even amid scores of backpacker eateries and shops catering to Western tourists, **New Day** (72 Ma May, tel. 04/3828-0315, www.newdayrestaurant.com, 10am-9pm daily, VND30,000-200,000) retains a strong local following. With a well-rounded menu that covers everything from pork, chicken, and beef to frog, duck, oysters, and vegetarian fare, New Day has reasonable prices.

Local institution Xoi Yen stays busy from morning to night.

Cha Ca La Vong (14 Cha Ca, tel. 04/3823-9875, 11am-2pm and 5:30pm-9pm daily, VND170,000) is the city's oldest restaurant, serving up sizzling pans of *cha ca* (pan-fried fish) since 1871. The modest, two-story spot specializes in only this dish, accompanied by rice noodles and peanuts. The portions are undersized and overpriced, though tasty. The staff is abrupt, but the restaurant is a popular stop. For better service and larger portions, **Cha Ca Thang Long** (21-31 Duong Thanh, tel. 04/3824-5115, www.cha-cathanglong.com, 10am-9pm daily, VND120,000) provides the same dish at a more reasonable price.

Com Ga (1 Cua Dong, tel. 04/3923-3728, comgacafe@gmail.com, 8am-11pm daily, VND55,000-180,000) sits on a busy corner along the western edge of the Old Quarter. The restaurant prides itself on its hearty helpings of the namesake *com ga* (Hoi An-style chicken and rice). The second-floor balcony makes an ideal spot for a drink and late-afternoon people-watching.

CATHEDRAL DISTRICT
Cafés and Bakeries

A large, comfy, Western-style shop, **Joma Bakery & Cafe** (22 Ly Quoc Su, tel. 04/3839-1619, www.joma.biz, 7am-9pm daily, VND30,000-180,000) offers a taste of home, with delicious breakfasts, sandwiches, bagels, European coffee, and mouthwatering pastries. Relax in the small seating area up front near the main counter, or head out back to the larger café, where cozy couches and quiet tables await. You'll also find another location at **Joma To Ngoc Van** (43 To Ngoc Van, tel. 04/3718-6071, www.joma.biz, 7am-9pm daily, VND30,000-180,000). Both outlets have delivery services. A portion of their sales go to local charitable organizations.

Just off the main drag, the storefront of **Loft Stop Cafe** (11B Bao Khanh, tel. 04/3928-9433, www.loft-stop-cafe.com, 8am-11pm daily, VND25,000-200,000) is lit up by two well-stocked display cases laden with decadent treats. Pastries, cakes, and other goodies attract more than a few visitors. Its cool, quiet, street-side digs offer some respite, and with a range of coffee, tea, and other beverages populating the menu, it's a good place to pop in for dessert or a mid-afternoon snack. The Loft Stop also makes a solid pizza.

International

The ★ **Hanoi Social Club** (6 Hoi Vu, tel. 04/3938-2117, 8am-11pm daily, VND95,000-170,000) dishes out an eclectic array of international fare, including burgers and breakfast foods alongside goulash, roti wraps, mango curry, and Moroccan chicken. Its chefs are able to adjust dishes for vegetarian, vegan, and gluten-free diners. The beverage menu is equally varied, including European coffees and teas as well as a few Vietnamese favorites, such as egg coffee and *ca phe sua da* (iced coffee with milk). Comfy chairs, whimsical decor, and indie music round out the Social Club's offerings. There is live music on evenings and weekends.

It's hard not to be charmed by the laid-back ambience and breezy second-floor balcony at classy **Buon Dua Le Cafe** (20 Hang Hanh, tel. 04/3825-7388, 6:30am-10:30pm daily, VND45,000-275,000). Down a quiet side street but close to Hoan Kiem Lake, the place is outfitted with polished wooden furniture and the artwork of local painter Duc Loi. The menu is mainly Vietnamese, with a few Western dishes. The open-air hangout makes a perfect place to start your day or kick back with a happy hour beverage as the sun goes down.

Street Food

After one bowl of rice porridge, called ★ *chao suon* (corner of Ly Quoc Su and Ngo Huyen, 7am-9pm daily, VND25,000/bowl), from the small, street-side outfit near St. Joseph's Cathedral, you'll be coming back for seconds. A smooth, stew-like consistency, this particular vendor's porridge is served with savory pork and *quay,* essentially a fried breadstick, on top. On the miniature plastic stools that line the road, sit and enjoy the bustle of the city while tucking into your piping hot *chao.* For extra flavor, toss in some black pepper. Portions are just right, making this a great breakfast or midday snack.

FRENCH QUARTER
French

La Badiane (10 Nam Ngu, tel. 04/3942-4509, www.labadiane-hanoi.com, 11:30am-2pm and 6pm-9:45pm Mon.-Sat., VND520,000-1,590,000) is the city's finest French restaurant. Venture through the restaurant's arching, vine-covered white corridor and you'll find a host of gourmet dishes, from lamb shank and duck breast, tartar and carpaccio to pan-fried foie gras, homemade pasta, and sumptuous desserts. Each meal is a work of art, carefully plated. Chef Benjamin Rascalou, a veteran of the Parisian restaurant circuit, keeps things interesting with a regularly changing menu.

Vegetarian

Hidden down an alley, **Nang Tam Com Chay** (79A Tran Hung Dao, tel. 04/3942-4140, 9am-9pm daily, VND25,000-100,000) is a popular Vietnamese vegetarian joint that features scores of meatless dishes, from standard tofu-and-tomato-sauce to mock-meat re-creations of traditional local fare. Tasty, filling set lunches go for as little as VND60,000. The small, air-conditioned dining area is usually full of locals at both lunch and dinner.

Vietnamese

Ngon (18 Phan Boi Chau, tel. 04/3942-8162, www.ngonhanoi.com.vn, 6:30am-9:30pm daily, VND45,000-360,000) and its extensive menu provide solid guidance on what to eat and how to eat it. Thanks to the place's market-style setup, diners are able to peruse everything before choosing. Set within a large courtyard, the bustling street food-style eatery is packed during lunch and evenings with tourists and locals. Delve into soups, sautés, spring rolls, and sauces.

BA DINH DISTRICT
Cafés and Bakeries

The folks at **Cong Caphe** (32 Dien Bien Phu, tel. 09/1181-1141, www.congcaphe.com, 7am-11pm daily, VND30,000-80,000) have taken the aesthetics of Vietnamese Communism and applied it to an urban coffee shop, with a decor featuring weathered wood, peeling paint, exposed brick, and stark concrete. The brown-paper menus list coffee, tea, and smoothies alongside coffee-coconut shakes and coffee with yogurt. There are other locations around town, including a spot on Nguyen Huu Huan (35A Nguyen Huu Huan, tel. 04/6292-5814, 7am-11pm daily). Cong occasionally hosts live music, during which time it serves a few alcoholic beverages.

International

A training restaurant and one of the most popular spots in town, ★ **KOTO** (59 Van Mieu, tel. 04/3747-0337, www.koto.com.au, 8am-10pm daily, VND85,000-300,000) has made an impact on the restaurant scene as well as the lives of its many graduates. Started in 1999, KOTO (Know One, Teach One) admits young disadvantaged Vietnamese into its two-year training program, which provides job training in the hospitality industry. The restaurant acts as a training ground for students while serving delicious renditions of both Vietnamese and international favorites. The eatery's location makes it conducive to a lunchtime visit, though things can get hectic around this time. Seating is spread out over four floors.

Many KOTO graduates have gone on to open their own restaurants, the most popular of which is **Pots 'n Pans** (57 Bui Thi Xuan, tel. 04/3944-0204, www.potsnpans.vn, 11am-11pm daily, VND210,000-690,000), an upmarket fusion spot with high-quality service and plenty of ambience. Though it's expensive, the food is truly a work of art; opt for one of the set menus, as these offer the best value.

Street Food

If you are near the Temple of Literature in the afternoon, swing by Ly Van Phuc, where you'll find finger-licking **barbecue chicken** (end of Ly Van Phuc, 4pm-late daily, VND6,000-10,000/piece) starting around 3pm-4pm. Snacks are pay-as-you-go, with varying prices for legs and wings. These tasty treats make the perfect *do nhau* (drinking food) to pair with a beer. Though there are several shops along this street, the ones at the far end are the best.

WEST LAKE AREA
Cafés and Bakeries

Saint Honore (5 Xuan Dieu, tel. 04/3933-2355, www.sainthonore.com.vn, 7am-10pm daily, VND35,000-200,000) is a charming little Parisian-style bistro, replete with flaky, decadent pastries, fresh bread, and a deli counter that wraps around the end of the building. Delicious sandwiches and crepes feature on the menu alongside a range of coffee and tea options; while there are a handful of more sophisticated meals on offer, it's best to stick to simpler fare, as this is where the café excels. Saint Honore also has a second location (31 Thai Phien, tel. 04/3974-9483, 6:30am-10pm daily) closer to downtown.

SELF-CATERING

Hanoian cuisine is as varied as it is delicious. Those with dietary issues, or those who simply prefer more control in the preparation of their meals, will appreciate shops like **Veggy's** (99 Xuan Dieu, tel. 04/3719-4630, 8am-8pm daily), a small but well-stocked grocery store near the northern end of West Lake that's packed with familiar Western brands like Kraft, Campbell's, and Betty Crocker. For even more selection, **Annam Gourmet** (51 Xuan Dieu, tel. 04/6673-9661, www.annam-gourmet.com, 7am-9pm daily), located in the Syrena Shopping Center, offers a range of useful cooking items and canned goods as well as a small bakery and deli counter, where you'll find several different types of cheese and cold cuts. Prices at both of these shops run on the high side, but you'll find many familiar brand names and a much larger selection than local supermarkets.

If you're simply looking for basic groceries and other essentials, the **Hapro Mart** (63 Cau Go, tel. 04/3266-9621, 8:30am-11:30pm daily) in the Old Quarter sells things like pasta, canned goods, and milk. While it's not very big, the store manages to cover most simple ingredients as well as a few toiletries and other odds and ends. There is also a second location (35 Hang Bong, 8:30am-10pm daily) nearby.

Accommodations

The bustling streets and narrow, snaking alleys of Hanoi's downtown districts hold accommodations to fit every budget, from basic dorm beds to palatial five-star suites. Base yourself within reach of Hoan Kiem Lake, as this will ensure a reasonable proximity to most of Hanoi's sights, restaurants, and shopping. With a reputation as one of the country's most walkable metropolises and a surplus of quality budget, mid-range, and high-end accommodations, there is no reason not to stay in the downtown area.

As travelers to the city will quickly learn, the Old Quarter is not a place for light sleepers. While there is no shortage of accommodations in Hanoi, several factors come into play when booking a room, not the least of which is noise level. Those with a tolerance for white noise or, at the very least, a set of earplugs will find no fault in the many rooms north of the lake; those who prefer more quiet may find peace down the web of alleys beside St. Joseph's Cathedral, where many of the cheaper budget accommodations have set up shop. A clutch of luxury hotels populates the French Quarter, many of them bearing unique historical significance in addition to high-end amenities and five-star service.

OLD QUARTER

This small but incredibly dense neighborhood manages to squeeze plenty of top-notch accommodations into a few blocks north of Hoan Kiem Lake, right in the center of the action. Prices run higher here while room sizes can be on the small side. Noise levels are higher than you might find elsewhere in the city.

Under VND210,000

Away from the spirited backpacker haunts, **Hanoi Hostel** (91C Hang Ma, tel. 04/6270-0006, www.vietnam-hostel.com, VND125,000 dorm, VND570,000 double) offers a peaceful place for weary budget travelers to lay their heads. The mixed and female dorms have clean, comfy beds and en suite bathrooms, personal lockers, daily breakfast, and a free happy-hour beer. The outfit in charge runs a tour service downstairs. While there's not really much of a common area, this hostel's location and laid-back vibe make up for that. There is also a second location (32 Hang Vai, tel. 04/6270-2009) nearby.

Hanoi Backpackers' Downtown (9 Ma May, tel. 04/3935-1891, www.vietnambackpackerhostels.com, VND185,000-340,000 dorm, VND1,150,000 double) is a good option for those in search of travel buddies, though if it's quiet you seek, then this is not the place to crash. Single mixed dorms, female-only rooms, and double bed dorms are available, all with personal lockers, air-conditioning, Wi-Fi, and communal bathrooms. Breakfast is served in the restaurant each morning. Though a few private rooms are available, you're better off going elsewhere if you'd prefer your own space.

VND210,000-525,000

Rooms at **Hanoi City Hostel** (95B Hang Ga, tel. 04/3828-1379, www.hanoicityhostel.com, VND360,000-410,000, breakfast included) are spacious and a bit worn but right for the price, counting hot water, air-conditioning, TV, Wi-Fi, a fridge, and tea- and coffee-making facilities among its standard amenities. Both front- and back-facing rooms are available, the former boasting large windows and lots of light, the latter offering more quiet away from the traffic noise of the downtown area. The staff can help arrange onward travel and transportation.

VND525,000-1,050,000

Though rooms at the **Rising Dragon Legend** (55 Hang Be, tel. 04/3935-2648, www.risingdragonhotel.com, VND790,000-1,585,000, breakfast included) are decidedly small, this skinny budget venture offers decent value for money, with clean, modern furnishings and comfy beds, hot water, air-conditioning, TV, minibar, in-room safe, Wi-Fi access, and tea- and coffee-making facilities. The hotel staff are a friendly and professional bunch who assist with travel bookings around northern Vietnam.

In a big and hectic city, the ★ **Hanoi Guesthouse** (85 Ma May, tel. 04/3935-2571, www.hanoiguesthouse.com, VND680,000-1,135,000, breakfast included) truly feels like a homier stay than most, with free refreshments on tap in the lobby and a notably attentive staff. Rooms are a great value, outfitted with TV, Wi-Fi, hot water, air-conditioning, a minibar, an in-room safe, and tea- and coffee-making facilities. Add-ons include airport transfer, travel bookings, laundry, and luggage storage.

Cozy, well-appointed, and right in the heart of the Old Quarter, rooms at the **Hanoi Old Town** (95 Hang Chieu, tel. 04/3929-0783, www.hanoioldtown.com, VND680,000-910,000, breakfast included) feature generously sized beds, hot water, television, air-conditioning, and Wi-Fi access. Facilities are older than other hotels in the area, but staff at the Old Town are a cheerful bunch and assist with travel services and tours around northern Vietnam. For lots of light and a street view, front-facing rooms are a solid choice; but if you prefer peace and quiet, opt for a spot at the back, where noise levels aren't so high.

★ **Golden Time Hostel 3** (106 Ma may, tel. 09/1779-3099, www.goldentimehostel.com, VND410,000-590,000) is a budget hotel, not a hostel. Its location north of Hoan Kiem Lake affords travelers a prime spot amid the action of the Old Quarter. Rooms are well-kept and come with television, air-conditioning, hot water, and Wi-Fi. Some rooms don't have windows. The staff is attentive and assists with transportation and travel bookings. For an equally worthy option more removed from the bustling downtown area, **Golden Time 1** (43 Ly Thai To, tel. 04/3935-1091, www.goldentimehostel.com, VND410,000-550,000) is on the eastern side of the lake. While there's less atmosphere here, good service and most of the same amenities apply.

VND1,050,000-2,100,000

Hugging the western edge of the Old Quarter, the **Charming Hotel 2** (31 Hang Ga, tel. 04/3923-4031, www.hanoicharminghotel.com, VND1,170,000-2,140,000, breakfast included) provides five-star service for a fraction of the price. Rooms are modern and well-appointed, with in-room amenities such as a computer, safe, work desk, TV, and Wi-Fi access, as well as complimentary water and tea- and coffee-making facilities. The hotel offers a handful of different room types, from standard superiors, with and without windows, to spacious executive accommodations.

The 25-room **Oriental Central Hotel** (39 Hang Bac, tel. 04/3935-1117, www.orientalcentralhotel.com, VND945,000-2,150,000, breakfast included) stands out thanks to top-notch staff and a modern look. Well-appointed rooms come with the standard amenities as well as complimentary daily water. The antique-style bronze showerheads and framed photographs of everyday Vietnamese scenes add to the ambience. The superior, deluxe, and suite rooms have varying degrees of natural light. Opt for at least a deluxe, as these afford a better view. Additional services like travel bookings and airport pickup can be arranged.

Calypso Suites Hotel (11E Trung Yen, Dinh Liet, tel. 04/3935-2753, www.calypsosuiteshotel.com, VND910,000-1,575,000, breakfast included), run by the same people as Oriental Central Hotel, bears a similar red, black, and white design scheme and equally conscientious service. Expect standard amenities as well as Wi-Fi, DVD players, and in-room safes. The hotel's alley location minimizes the noise of the Old Quarter.

The **Essence Hanoi Hotel** (22 Ta Hien, tel. 04/3935-2485, www.essence-hanoihotel.com, VND1,365,000-2,605,000, breakfast included) provides quality service and posh, mid-range boutique rooms that feature in-room computers, in-room safes, and daily complimentary water on top of the standard amenities. The hotel's restaurant operates throughout the day on an à la carte menu. Services such as laundry, luggage storage, and tour bookings can be arranged at reception. Rooms vary in size and access to natural light; take a step up from the most basic option for a room with a view.

Part of the Elegance chain, ★ **Hanoi La Siesta Diamond Hotel** (32 Lo Su, tel. 04/3935-1632, www.hanoielegancehotel.com, VND1,400,000-2,490,000) is one of the company's best properties. Perched on the edge of the Old Quarter, the Diamond houses boutique rooms and the Gourmet Corner, a much-touted top-floor restaurant with pleasant lake views, as well as an outdoor terrace bar. Rooms feature a simple but elegant decor, plush beds, an in-room safe, computer, and complimentary water alongside the usual amenities.

The grand **Tirant Hotel** (36-38 Gia Ngu, tel. 04/6269-8899, www.tirant-hotel.com, VND1,575,000-3,045,000) boasts a larger property than much of its Old Quarter competition, no easy feat in this packed neighborhood. Above the lavish reception area, 63 well-appointed rooms are outfitted in regal furnishings and come with an in-room computer, minibar, and tea- and coffee-making facilities in addition to standard hotel amenities. Breakfast is served in the hotel's downstairs restaurant each morning. A lake-view lounge tops the building, affording pleasant views of Hoan Kiem Lake. You'll find a fitness center and a small swimming pool here, as well as a travel desk, which assists with transportation and tour bookings.

CATHEDRAL DISTRICT

Situated just north of St. Joseph's Cathedral is a tiny backpacker enclave on Ngo Huyen that provides decent rooms at lower prices than in the Old Quarter.

Under VND210,000

The original ★ **Hanoi Backpackers'** (48 Ngo Huyen, tel. 04/3828-5372, www.vietnambackpackerhostels.com, VND115,000-140,000 dorm, VND575,000-670,000 double, breakfast included) sits about halfway down narrow Ngo Huyen, a stone's throw from the Cathedral and Hoan Kiem

Lake. Both mixed and all-female beds are available, with hot water, Wi-Fi, air-conditioning, and personal lockers. While there are a handful of private rooms, it's better to look elsewhere for quiet, because the crowd here likes to party. The staff can help arrange onward travel and transportation.

It's a little less tidy than Hanoi Backpackers', but **Central Backpackers** (16 Ly Quoc Su, tel. 04/3938-1849, www.centralbackpackershostel.com, VND115,000-140,000 dorm, breakfast included) is an affordable option. Mixed dorms are outfitted with personal lockers, air-conditioning, and Wi-Fi, with hot water in the shared bathrooms. During happy hour, you can enjoy a daily free beer. This is a good backpacker spot. The private rooms are not worthwhile; for peace and quiet, look elsewhere.

VND210,000-525,000

Especen Hotel (28 Tho Xuong, tel. 04/3824-4401, www.especen.vn, VND370,000-510,000) offers clean, spacious rooms in the heart of the Cathedral District. Tucked down an alley, the hotel is a five-minute walk from Hoan Kiem Lake. Rooms offer single- or queen-size beds and come equipped with a television, air-conditioning, Wi-Fi, and hot water. Long-term stays can be arranged for a discounted rate, and the friendly hotel staff can assist with travel plans around the city as well as throughout the north. There are a number of copycats in the area that have duplicated the hotel's sign. Go to this exact address to avoid impostors.

The **Bluebell Hotel** (41 Ngo Huyen, tel. 04/3938-2398, www.hanoibluebellhotel.com, VND320,000-390,000), hidden among the clutch of budget accommodations beside the cathedral, is one of this alley's better options, offering clean and well-priced rooms kitted out with hot water, air-conditioning, tea- and coffee-making facilities, fridge, TV, and Wi-Fi. If you're willing to hike up a few flights of stairs, the higher floors are better, as they tend to minimize the noise. All rooms are well-appointed and the friendly staff can assist with travel bookings and transportation.

Tucked tightly down an alley off the road circling Hoan Kiem Lake, **Little Hanoi Hostel 2** (32 Le Thai To, tel. 04/3928-9897, www.littlehanoihostel.com, VND455,000-550,000 double, breakfast included) is a pleasant surprise. Quaint, quiet, and incredibly close to the water, this mini-hotel's location eliminates much of the noise problem that comes with being downtown. It boasts cozy, well-kept accommodations that count air-conditioning, hot water, Wi-Fi access, TV, and natural light among their amenities. The staff are a cheerful bunch, willing to help with transportation and travel arrangements, as well as city recommendations.

Though it's a little aged, **Tung Trang** (13 Tam Thuong, tel. 04/3828-6267, tungtranghotel@yahoo.com, VND405,000-1,057,000) stands out for its peaceful location, nestled amid a tangle of alleys just off Hang Bong. Rooms are basic, featuring hot water, air-conditioning, TV, and Wi-Fi access, all complemented nicely by the hospitality of the staff. Front rooms are spacious and include balconies, while smaller, cheaper accommodations are also available.

VND525,000-1,050,000

The most affordable in a chain of well-run, family-owned accommodations, **Splendid Star Grand Hotel** (14 Tho Xuong, tel. 04/3938-1435, www. grand.splendidstarhotel.com, VND685,000-1,480,000, breakfast included) features bright, comfortable rooms with hot water, air-conditioning, TV, Wi-Fi access, complimentary water, an in-room safe, minibar, tea- and coffee-making facilities, and a DVD player. The staff can help arrange onward travel and transportation.

Decked out in miniature chandeliers, plush carpet, and snakeskin wallpaper, the **Angel Palace Hotel** (173 Hang Bong, tel. 04/6299-8666, www. angelpalacehotel.com.vn, VND795,000-1,700,000, breakfast included) makes a statement with its style as well as its service. All accommodations are modern and well-appointed, counting hot water, air-conditioning, TV, Wi-Fi access, complimentary water, a writing desk, and tea- and coffee-making facilities in the standard list of amenities. Additional services, such as laundry and tour arrangements, can be made with the friendly and professional folks at the front desk.

VND1,050,000-2,100,000

Tried and trusted, the **Hanoi City Palace Hotel** (106 Hang Bong, tel. 04/3938-2333, www.hanoicitypalacehotel.com, VND1,135,000-1,700,000, breakfast included) boasts top-notch service and a chic decor that exceeds the level of most mid-range accommodations. Rooms at this charming boutique hotel feature spacious bathrooms as well as a work desk, minibar, television, in-room safe, tea- and coffee-making facilities, and complimentary water. Suite rooms include a private balcony. Additional touches like a welcome drink and fruit platter highlight the staff's attention to detail. The hotel runs a travel desk, which assists with tours around the city and beyond.

FRENCH QUARTER

The chic French Quarter is home to the city's most historic and high-end hotels. From the world-famous Metropole to elegant modern hotels like Nikko, Hotel de l'Opera, and Hilton Hanoi Opera, this is a neighborhood for the more affluent traveler.

Over VND2,100,000

The spectacular, stately ★ **Sofitel Legend Metropole** (15 Ngo Quyen, tel. 04/3826-6919, www.sofitel.com, VND6,910,000-46,095,000) opened in 1901. Its historic white building, with black shutters and stocky balustrades, earned a reputation as the finest hotel in Indochina, catering to famous visitors and well-to-do residents. The five-star opulence of the Metropole is evident in its plush, sophisticated rooms, which come with a television and complimentary bottled water. The hotel boasts a pair of luxurious restaurants, a spa, swimming pool, gift shop, sauna, and fitness center.

The five-star **Hilton Hanoi Opera** (1 Le Thanh Tong, tel. 04/3933-0500, www.hanoi.hilton.com, VND2,000,000-22,000,000) stands just south of the city's historic theater and exudes class from its regal, vaulted reception hall all the way to the elegant, well-appointed guest rooms. Accommodations feature standard hotel amenities alongside a minibar, in-room safe, Internet access, and tea- and coffee-making facilities. A fitness center, outdoor pool, sports bar, two restaurants, and a swanky café round out the hotel's offerings.

An imposing white building, the plush **Nikko Hotel** (84 Tran Nhan Tong, tel. 04/3822-3535, www.hotelnikkohanoi.com.vn, VND2,310,000-12,495,000, breakfast included) boasts 257 guest rooms, ranging from deluxe rooms to park view and executive lodgings and suites. Outfitted with high-quality amenities such as television, Wi-Fi access, a spacious bathroom, and a small sitting alcove, all rooms are well-appointed and come with use of the hotel swimming pool, whirlpool tub, and fitness center. The Nikko counts a spa, a bar, and three restaurants in its offerings.

A cross between cozy guesthouse and high-end hotel, the **Hilton Garden Inn** (20 Phan Chu Trinh, tel. 04/3944-9396, www.hiltongardeninn3.hilton.com, VND2,000,000-4,200,000) provides a more casual approach to luxury accommodation, with B&B-style lodgings alongside five-star service. Room amenities include television, Wi-Fi access, an in-room safe, desk, refrigerator, and tea- and coffee-making facilities, as well as use of the business center and gym. A bar, restaurant, and 24-hour pantry market round out the inn's additional services.

The **Hotel de l'Opera** (29 Trang Tien, tel. 04/6282-5555, www.hoteldelopera.com, VND4,450,000-8,100,000) is not the first five-star hotel to grace this spot. At the turn of the 20th century, an elegant building known as the Hanoi Hotel served as a popular meeting place for local socialites. That building was eventually torn down in 2004 and rebuilt. Now outfitted with bold decor and first-class facilities, including flat-screen television and Wi-Fi access, the hotel stands out for its unique design, furnished in vivid, eye-catching colors. The chic, ground-floor **Cafe Lautrec** is a posh and popular French Quarter dining spot.

Tucked between high-rise office buildings and sprawling department stores, the **De Syloia** (17A Tran Hung Dao, tel. 04/3824-5346, www.desyloia.com, VND2,265,000-3,100,000, breakfast included) is a cozy boutique hotel modeled after a colonial-style villa. Each well-appointed room comes with Wi-Fi access, TV, an in-room safe, minibar, and complimentary water. Guests have access to the hotel's gym and business center. De Syloia's restaurant, Cay Cau, features both Vietnamese cuisine and live traditional music nightly from 7pm.

WEST LAKE

West Lake, with a handful of secluded high-end hotels, is the quietest neighborhood in the capital city. Xuan Dieu, the street bordering the eastern edge of the water, features several nice restaurants and bars, though options are limited.

Over VND2,100,000

Well removed from the chaos of downtown, the **Sheraton Hanoi** (11 Xuan Dieu, tel. 04/3719-9000, www.sheratonhanoi.com, VND2,100,000-34,000,000) sits just over two miles from the Old Quarter and has a pool, spa, garden, opulent lobby, and several restaurants on its sprawling lake shore property. Guest rooms feature the standard hotel amenities as well as a minibar, fridge, in-room safe, complimentary water, and tea- and coffee-making facilities.

Off the eastern shore of the lake, **InterContinental Hanoi West Lake** (5 Tu Hoa, tel. 04/6270-8888, www.hanoi.intercontinental.com, VND4,068,000-34,000,000) boasts over 300 guest rooms, including stunning over-water pavilions connected to the water's edge by a maze of floating walkways. Plush rooms are outfitted with a fusion of traditional Asian-inspired elements and modern decor, and include Wi-Fi access and a private balcony. The hotel's three restaurants serve a range of international and Vietnamese cuisine. The outdoor pool and a state-of-the-art fitness center are free for guests to use.

Nestled between West Lake and Truc Bach, the **Pan Pacific Hanoi** (1 Thanh Nien, tel. 04/3823-8888, www.panpacific.com, VND2,700,000-9,500,000) is blessed with attractive natural surroundings. The Sofitel's location brings travelers closer to the heart of the city while still providing peace and quiet. The five-star hotel boasts 273 guest rooms outfitted with plush modern decor, an in-room safe, Wi-Fi access, and a flat-screen television. A pair of posh restaurants showcase Chinese, Western, and Vietnamese cuisine, while the Summit Lounge overlooks the lake. A swimming pool, spa, and fitness center are part of the Sofitel's offerings.

Information and Services

TOURIST INFORMATION

You'll find scores of travel agencies boasting "free tourist information" around the Old Quarter, but this local wisdom extends no further than a brochure of the company's tour packages. Your hotel is usually the best place to seek out unbiased travel tips, not to mention other extras like free maps. If you can't seem to track these down, the **Tourist Information Center** (7 Dinh Tien Hoang, tel. 04/3926-3370, www.ticvietnam.vn, 8am-9pm daily) opposite the northern edge of Hoan Kiem Lake provides detailed plans of the city as well as a complimentary Hanoi guide, which lists recommendations on hotels, restaurants, sights, and other attractions in town. While the company operating this office sells its own tours, the free materials on offer make the place a little more helpful than most.

BANKS AND CURRENCY EXCHANGE

You'll find ATMs on nearly every street corner in Hanoi, particularly in the downtown area.

Most hotels and tour agencies offer to exchange currency, as do the majority of banks in the downtown area. Look up the actual exchange rate to ensure that you receive a fair conversion. If you're pressed for time, the bank is your best bet.

Most banks in the capital are open 8am-5pm Monday-Friday. Vietnamese institutions like **Vietcombank** (www.vietcombank.com.vn) and **Sacombank** (www.sacombank.com.vn) tend to take a lunch break during the day, shutting their doors 11:30am-1pm; foreign companies like **HSBC** (www.hsbc.com.vn), **Citibank** (www.citibank.com.vn), and **ANZ** (www.anz.com) stay open all day. Some Vietnamese banks are open on Saturday mornings.

While much of the country remains cash-only, some places in Hanoi, including high-end hotels and upscale restaurants, accept credit cards as a form of payment. This is the exception rather than the rule, so check ahead of time. Many businesses tack on a small additional charge for using plastic over paper money.

INTERNET AND POSTAL SERVICES

Hanoi's **international post office** (6 Dinh Le, tel. 04/3825-4503, www.vnpost.vn, 7am-5pm Mon.-Fri., 8am-5pm Sat.-Sun.) staffs English-speaking employees. For additional services, visit the **central post office** (75 Dinh Tien Hoang, tel. 04/3825-5948, www.vnpost.vn, 7:30am-6:30pm Mon.-Fri., 8:30am-5:30pm Sat.-Sun.) just next door. You are less likely to find an English speaker, but employees will usually point you in the right direction.

When shipping packages, Hanoi offers three options: the local post, often slow and less reliable, though affordable, or **UPS** (10 Le Thach, tel. 04/3824-6483, www.ups.com, 7:30am-6pm Mon.-Sat.), and **DHL** (Le Thach,

the Vietcombank ATM on Cau Go

tel. 01/800-1530, www.dhl.com, 8am-noon and 1pm-6pm Mon.-Fri.). Both shipping companies have offices on the northern side of the central post office, just around the corner from its front door. Unless absolutely necessary, avoid international shipping, as costs quickly add up.

You'd be hard-pressed to find a hotel in town that does not have a desktop computer in the hotel lobby or, at the very least, a Wi-Fi connection. Indeed, most cafés and restaurants offer free wireless Internet for paying customers.

PHONE SERVICE

Many travelers buy a local cell phone for the trip. SIM cards and basic, reliable Nokia phones are widely available, both new and secondhand, from electronics shops around the Old Quarter as well as at **The Gioi Di Dong** (468-472 Le Duan, tel. 1/800-1060, www.thegioididong.com, 8am-10pm daily), with the cheapest options beginning around VND350,000. Once you obtain a phone and SIM card, you'll have to purchase mobile credit, which is found at most local *tap hoa* (convenience stores). The three main cell carriers in Vietnam are Vinaphone, Mobifone, and Viettel, all of whom operate on a pay-as-you-go basis. Credit comes in increments of VND20,000, VND50,000, VND100,000, and VND200,000.

EMERGENCY AND MEDICAL SERVICES

Vietnam employs three separate phone numbers for emergency response services: 113 is meant for police assistance in the event of robberies, traffic accidents, and crime-related incidents; 114 links to the city's firefighters; and 115 covers medical emergencies. None of these hotlines are likely to have an English speaker on the other end and the city's emergency response teams are sluggish at best.

In the event of a medical emergency, the best thing you can do is contact a foreign medical center directly for help. Local facilities like **Hong Ngoc Hospital** (55 Yen Ninh, tel. 04/3927-5568, www.hongngochospital.vn, 8am-5pm daily) are reliable for simple aches and pains. International hospitals such as **Family Medical Practice** (298 Kim Ma, Van Phuc Compound, tel. 04/3843-0748, www.vietnammedicalpractice.com), which staffs experienced English-speaking foreign and Vietnamese doctors, stay open 24 hours and assist with more serious predicaments. **International SOS** (51 Xuan Dieu, tel. 04/3934-0666, www.internationalsos.com) provides a similar level of quality, though its pricing can run high.

PHARMACIES

Scores of pharmacies, also known as *nha thuoc tay,* are scattered throughout the Old Quarter and across town. These facilities stock prescription and over-the-counter remedies, as well as products like tampons and contact lens solution. Most downtown pharmacies also employ at least one English-speaking staff member. The **pharmacy** (119 Hang Gai, tel. 04/3828-6782,

7:30am-10pm daily) located on Hang Gai is a reliable option, as are the
several businesses that run along Phu Doan near the cathedral.

DIPLOMATIC SERVICES

While there is a **U.S. Embassy** (7 Lang Ha, tel. 04/3850-5000, www.viet-nam.usembassy.gov), all inquiries regarding American citizens must be directed to the Rose Garden Building, where **consular services** (Rose Garden Bldg., 170 Ngoc Khanh, 2nd Fl., tel. 04/3850-5000, www.vietnam.usembassy.gov, 8:30am-11:30am and 1pm-3:30pm Mon.-Thurs., by appt. only) are carried out, around the corner from the embassy. Due to the fact that all visitors must have a scheduled appointment on the books, look at the embassy's website ahead of time in order to discern what you'll need before venturing to this area. Appointments can also be made online. For emergencies, American citizens are advised to contact the embassy and consular services (tel. 04/3850-5000) during business hours; outside of these times, contact the embassy's **emergency hotline** (tel. 04/3520-4200) for assistance.

LAUNDRY

The majority of Hanoi's accommodations provide laundry services at an additional cost, and there is usually a markup for going this route. Standard pricing on the street is around VND25,000 per kilo, while you'll pay upwards of VND35,000 for the convenience of going through your hotel. The turnaround is usually about a day's time; in lousy winter weather be prepared to wait a little longer, as dryers are seldom used and the cold, humid winter months tend to leave everything a little damp.

Getting There

AIR

Flights from around the country and across the globe arrive at Hanoi's **Noi Bai International Airport** (HAN, Phu Minh ward, Soc Son district, tel. 04/3886-5047, www.noibaiairport.vn), 20 miles north of the city. Several budget airlines, including Jetstar, Air Asia, and Viet Jet, pass through here in addition to a host of other international carriers. Customs and immigration procedures move quickly; those completing pre-approved visa processing should expect to wait in line for a short while before passing through customs inspections. Those traveling domestically from other in-country destinations will be spared this waiting.

Once you've exited the airport, it's about a 45-minute ride into the city by taxi, minibus, or public bus. Many hotels can arrange airport pickup for an additional fee (starting at VND350,000), so long as you contact them in advance.

Taxis from the Airport

The airport is notorious for a host of taxi troubles: drivers quote flat rates that border on extortion or insist that the destination you've presented is closed, full, or for some other reason unavailable in hopes of steering you to another hotel, where they usually receive a kickback. When metered vehicles are available, it is not uncommon for meters to run up the fare at lightning speed. Your best bet is to write down the name and exact address of your hotel before leaving the airport. This way, you have a clear destination to show your driver and, should he or she attempt to take you elsewhere, you are able to politely refuse and point to the place on the paper.

The easiest way to procure a cab from the airport is to walk to the taxi stand (easily visible when leaving the arrivals area), where a flat rate (to downtown) will be posted on the sign out front. Once you have a taxi, confirm again with your driver the exact price as some drivers will still attempt to overcharge. Stick to trusted companies like **Mailinh Airport** (tel. 04/3822-2666). From the airport to the downtown area should cost no more than VND400,000, but sometimes even the most reputable companies are dishonest.

Airport Minibus

An airport **minibus** (tel. 04/3884-0496, www.nasco.vn, 5am-7:30pm daily, VND40,000), courtesy of Vietnam Airlines, leaves from Noi Bai when it has enough passengers to make the journey worthwhile, usually every 30 minutes or so. The minibus drops passengers off in front of the Vietnam Airlines office downtown, one block south of Hoan Kiem Lake. While you may have to wait a few minutes at the airport, this is by far the cheapest and most hassle-free option if you are traveling light. Even if your hotel is not within walking distance of the minibus stop, the combined cost of the minibus fare and a cab from downtown Hanoi to your final destination will be less expensive and reduce the risk of being overcharged by a taxi.

Noi Bai International Airport

The same minibuses also travel the reverse route back to the airport, leaving from the Vietnam Airlines office (corner of Quang Trung and Hai Ba Trung). There's no need to buy a ticket in advance; just hop on.

Public Bus from the Airport

A **public bus** (VND9,000) also makes a trip into town from the airport. **Bus number 17** travels via the Chuong Duong Bridge and lets off at Long Bien station, in between Hoan Kiem and West Lake, opposite a stretch of the city's ceramic wall. From here, it's less than a mile to the Old Quarter, making the rest of the journey easily walkable, depending upon your luggage; it's just as easy to catch a cab from here. **Bus number 7** also departs from Noi Bai, traveling to the western suburbs of the city. For more specific directions to your destination, it's possible to double-check your route with Google Maps, as its representation of the Hanoi public bus system is accurate and far easier than attempting to decipher the route listings on the Hanoi Bus website.

TRAIN

Hanoi's mammoth **train station** (120 Le Duan, tel. 04/3942-3697, www. gahanoi.com.vn, 8am-5pm daily) serves southern cities like Danang, Nha Trang, and Saigon, in addition to offering an overnight service north to Sapa. Tickets can be purchased through the station directly as well as from the station's website, and they are offered at travel agencies across town. Ask around when booking through a travel agency, as some outfits charge an excessive commission.

Taxis from the Train Station

The train station attracts plenty of cab drivers eager to catch a fare from an unsuspecting or weary traveler, often at several times the actual price. Opt for one of the **Mailinh** (tel. 04/3833-3333) cabs waiting out front. If you

Hanoi's train station

can't find a Mailinh cab, find a driver who will agree upon a fixed price, as rapid-fire taxi meters can turn a few dollars into 10 or 20 before you know it. Expect to pay around VND50,000 for a trip from the train station to Hoan Kiem Lake (10-minute ride). If you can't find someone willing to take a flat rate, walk a block or two away from the station and you'll find that drivers become increasingly more reasonable.

BUS

Hanoi has four separate bus stations scattered around the outskirts of the city. **Giap Bat** (Giai Phong, tel. 04/3864-1467, 5am-6pm daily) handles all routes heading south to destinations such as Ninh Binh and Hue, while vehicles at **Luong Yen** (Nguyen Khoai, tel. 04/3972-0477, 6am-11pm daily) and **Gia Lam** (9 Ngo Gia Kham, tel. 04/3827-1529, 5am-5pm daily) depart for Ha Long and Haiphong on a regular basis. To the west, **My Dinh** (20 Pham Hung, tel. 04/3768-5549, 4:30am-11pm daily) offers the occasional fare to Lao Cai and other northwestern towns, too.

You can eliminate the hassle of getting out to the station and navigating Vietnamese bus timetables and fare collectors by taking one of the comfy, air-conditioned coach buses that leave from the offices of **Sinh Tourist** (52 Luong Ngoc Quyen, tel. 04/3926-1568, www.thesinhtourist.vn, 7am-9pm daily) as well as several other local companies, all of which are located in the downtown area. Sinh Tourist has only the Luong Ngoc Quyen location and another on Tran Nhat Duat (64 Tran Nhat Duat, tel. 04/3929-0394, 7am-9pm daily). All other signs advertising "Sinh Cafe," "The Sinh Cafe," or "Sinh Cafe Tourist" are impostors. Go to the correct address and look for the blue-and-white logo.

Hoang Long (28 Tran Nhat Duat, tel. 04/3928-2828, www.hoanglon-gasia.com, 7:30am-7pm daily) also offers good value tickets. The company has satellite offices at the Luong Yen, Giap Bat, and My Dinh bus stations as well as its Old Quarter office.

Taxis from the Bus Station

If taxis from the airport come with a bad reputation, the cabs loitering outside of bus stations across the city are in an equally poor standing. Before you even step off the bus, there will be a swarm of drivers crowding the vehicle's entrance, just waiting for a tired, confused, or unsuspecting tourist to wander their way. The best thing you can do when stepping off a bus is grab your luggage and beeline for the exit. Ignore the touts, cab drivers, *xe om,* and anyone else who insists upon giving you a ride and walk to the street. From there, you needn't head more than a block before you find that cab drivers have backed off the hard sell, and it's much easier to pick out a reputable vehicle, insist upon a reasonable metered cab, and set off.

MOTORBIKE

As it rolls into the capital, Vietnam's famous Highway 1 goes by a few different names before splitting in two directions to avoid the city altogether;

from here, Ngoc Hoi transitions into Giai Phong and eventually Le Duan, landing you squarely in the heart of town just a few miles from Hoan Kiem Lake. For those arriving from the east, a pair of equally hectic national roads, Highway 14 and Highway 1, come together eight miles outside of the city and head across the Chuong Duong Bridge into town. Travelers from the west will follow Highway 6 directly to the city center, while those coming from the north have a few options. Thang Long Boulevard reaches Hanoi from the northwest, heading in toward Hoan Kiem Lake; there is also an airport road that passes by West Lake before approaching the city from the north. Being an obvious center of activity, no one highway is less crowded than the others. If possible, arrive before or after the evening rush hour.

Getting Around

Hanoi's traffic is hectic. Only confident, experienced drivers should brave Hanoian traffic. Much of the Old Quarter lacks streetlights or stop signs. Narrow roads combined with fast-paced driving can easily result in accidents. Many streets in downtown Hanoi are one way, and turning right on red is forbidden in the capital city.

TAXIS

Taxis in the capital have a less-than-stellar reputation for overcharging tourists, either through hyperactive meters or by making a few extra turns to run up the fare. Companies like **Mailinh** (tel. 04/3833-3333) and the red-and-blue **Taxi Group** (tel. 04/3857-5757) are reputable. When hailing a cab downtown, move away from the heavily touristed areas like Ma May or Ly Quoc Su and hop in a taxi near the main road instead, as this will decrease your chances of encountering an opportunist cabbie. Taxis should always be metered; while some drivers attempt to quote a flat rate, these are almost

rush hour traffic

never in your favor and so it's best to stick to the machine. If possible, try to pay with exact change or something close to it, as cab drivers often insist that they don't have small bills in hopes of gleaning a few extra thousand dong from you. Should you find yourself in a situation where you feel as though you're being taken advantage of—the meter is running too high, for example—stop the cab where you are, pay the fare, and exit the vehicle. Protesting or waiting to negotiate a price may result in more trouble.

RIDE-HAILING APPS

In the last couple years, both global giant **Uber** (www.uber.com) and the regional **Grab** (www.grab.com) have made their mark on Hanoi's traffic, much to the ire of traditional *xe om* drivers and cabbies alike. Both apps offer riders dirt-cheap rates in two- and four-wheeled vehicles. While Grab and Uber drivers can be a mixed bag—your driver might be a knowledge-able local, a whiz with GPS, or someone who just moved to the city yesterday—the service is generally safe and the prices are unbeatable. Unlike some other cities, you can also opt to pay by card or in cash.

XE OM

Walking around the Old Quarter, you will soon become accustomed to the waving hands and calls of "Hello! Motorbike!" that follow travelers around the city. *Xe om* drivers perch on most corners in the downtown area and can be relentless in their sales pitch. Agree upon a fare before hopping on board. From the Old Quarter to most tourist destinations in the area (barring faraway sights like the Museum of Ethnology and West Lake), your fare should not exceed VND50,000. If a particular driver is not willing to budge on the price, find another driver.

The folks that work Hanoi's *xe om* are daredevils, weaving through a hectic web of traffic that hurtles haphazardly down the narrow streets of downtown Hanoi. For safety's sake, insist upon wearing a helmet. Even if most Vietnamese helmets are not up to Western standards, better to have a little protection in the event of an accident than none at all.

CYCLOS

Slow-moving and seemingly less dangerous than their motorized compatriots, cyclos are the vehicle of choice for many travelers, as they give you the opportunity to sit back as you ply the streets of downtown Hanoi without fear of being run over by a motorbike or moving so quickly that your only thoughts are of safely making it to a particular destination. These sluggish, human-powered trikes ferry tourists all over the Old Quarter with occasional jaunts out to the French Quarter or Ba Dinh Square and beyond, depending on the passenger's needs. A standard cyclo trip lasts about an hour, weaving through the narrow downtown streets and allowing you to get a genuine feel of the city without the anxiety of tackling Hanoian traffic on your own. You'll have to bargain for your fare; most hour-long journeys begin around VND100,000. Your driver will be cycling you around with

his own two legs, and so you should expect to pay more than you would
for a motorized trip.

PUBLIC TRANSPORTATION
Bus
Hanoi's **public bus** (tel. 04/3843-6393, www.hanoibus.com.vn, 5am-9pm daily, VND7,000) lines run all over town and are the most cost-effective way to navigate its narrow streets. While maps of the entire system are not readily available, Google Maps accurately plots the city's bus routes, which makes finding the right bus line as easy as plugging your start and end destinations into the website. On the street, all stops are clearly marked with a blue sign bearing the bus number and its route, and fares are posted on the outside of each vehicle. Most rides around the city cost VND7,000. From the northern edge of Hoan Kiem Lake, buses 9 and 14 are especially useful, as these stop either directly in front of or not far from several popular sights, including Ho Chi Minh Mausoleum, the Temple of Literature, the Hanoi Flag Tower, and the Museum of Ethnology. While many of the more common downtown bus routes stop service at 9pm, some stop earlier, around 8pm. Both Google Maps and the Hanoi Bus website have accurate information regarding bus run times.

Electric Car
Dong Xuan Market runs an **electric car service** (north side of Hoan Kiem Lake, tel. 04/3929-0509, dongxuantours@gmail.com, 8am-10pm daily, VND200,000 for 35 min., VND300,000 for an hour) that ferries tourists around Hoan Kiem Lake and the Old Quarter area. A handful of standard routes are available, stopping at some of the city's more noteworthy landmarks and shopping areas. Electric cars seat a maximum of seven people and, while it is possible to travel with less than seven to a car, you'll have

Cyclo rides tend to be more relaxed than motorized *xe om* trips.

to cover the cost for the entire vehicle regardless of how few or how many individuals are on board.

VEHICLES FOR HIRE

Motorbike rentals are widely available in the downtown area, especially around Ngo Huyen near St. Joseph's Cathedral and along Dinh Liet to the north of Hoan Kiem Lake. Some of the foreign-owned rental outfits attempt to charge as much as VND210,000 per day, but you can easily rent a bike of reasonable quality for VND100,000 from one of the Vietnamese shops nearby. There are a handful of outfits on Dinh Liet that rent out vehicles at reasonable prices. Some shops may request collateral for the vehicle, in the form of either an ID or a cash deposit. Do a lap around the block and check for any issues before setting off for the day and insist upon a helmet for the trip. Though you'll see plenty of locals flaunting this rule, Vietnamese law requires that all drivers wear a helmet when driving.

Vicinity of Hanoi

Beyond the city limits, Hanoi's suburbs and surrounding countryside offer a few easygoing day trips. At the heart of the Red River Delta, a pair of booming traditional handicraft villages complement the urban chaos, while a serene pagoda complex southwest of the city affords an altogether different view of northern Vietnam. Jaunts to Tam Coc and Hoa Lu, Ninh Binh's main attractions, are possible, with plenty of tour providers offering day trips to the area.

PERFUME PAGODA

One of over 30 pagodas dotting the mountains of Ha Tay province, the beautifully austere **Perfume Pagoda (Chua Huong)** (www.lehoichuahuong.vn,

Perfume Pagoda

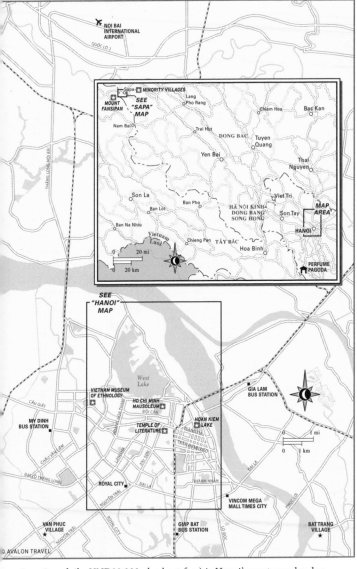

8am-5pm daily, VND80,000 plus boat fare) is Hanoi's most popular day trip destination. Perfume Pagoda, named for the clouds of incense permeating the cave's interior, is located inside a cave at the top of a mountain. Forty miles west of the capital, the pagoda complex sprawls across a series of hills overlooking the Yen River and is considered northern Vietnam's most important Buddhist center of worship. Though it's become increasingly more commercial, with the usual roving vendors and boat drivers, the scenery and famous incense-filled grotto are worth a visit for those looking to escape the city.

Most trips to Perfume Pagoda are done via all-inclusive tour, as this is the most hassle-free way to visit. Tour outfitters transport passengers to Yen Vy, a boat station in the town of Huong Son. From here, travelers board a small wooden **rowboat** (VND50,000/person). The boat glides on a small river past craggy limestone mountains and dense forest, taking about an hour from end to end. When your vessel reaches the pagoda complex, venture through the impressive three-door gate, a stark, towering structure whose black Chinese characters stand out against a bright white background. Past the gates, the temple Chua Thien Tru, also known as Heaven's Kitchen, houses a statue of Quan Am. It's one of the more atmospheric pagodas in the north.

The highlight of the pagoda complex is Huong Tich Cave, which is 164 feet above the water's edge atop a mountain. Though you have the option of reaching Huong Tich on foot, following a winding path up the mountain, most visitors prefer to jump in a bright yellow cable car (VND100,000 one-way, VND160,000 round-trip) to the mouth of the cave, where a set of stone steps descends into the darkened grotto. The cave interior is filled with small altars, obscured by an incense haze, and lacquer effigies. Once you've wandered through, walk back down toward the river. The steps become treacherous in foul weather; you can also hop on the cable car for the return trip. Respectful dress is a must at the complex.

While it's possible to reach the complex on your own via motorbike, the hassle of urban traffic is not really worth the few dollars you might save. Moreover, the journey to Perfume Pagoda is not nearly as picturesque as the sight itself. Dozens of tour companies in Hanoi offer full-day excursions that include transportation, entry fees, lunch, and a guide for as little as VND530,000.

HANDICRAFT VILLAGES

Across Vietnam, dozens of villages lay claim to culinary specialties or unique traditional crafts. These small, tight-knit communities have produced marble statues, fine silk, traditional Vietnamese lacquerware, or handmade pottery for centuries. Just outside of Hanoi, Bat Trang to the south and Van Phuc to the west each boast a long tradition of producing top-quality items and are known throughout Vietnam for their skilled craftspeople.

Bat Trang

Ten miles south and across the Red River, the small village of **Bat Trang** has been making high-quality ceramics since the 15th century and is a popular stop for shoppers in search of ceramics. Today, its pottery is nationally famous and exported around the world, with modern-day potters crafting both the traditional blue-and-white ceramics of the past as well as more colorful contemporary designs. Price tags in some of the larger outlets tend not to vary much from those in the city, but you'll find that there is more room for bargaining here and seemingly endless variety.

Most shops (which are also people's houses) are open around 7am-5pm or 6pm daily, and vendors sell similar objects. Visiting Bat Trang is like perusing a large pottery market.

Often, shops will have someone working on pottery, giving a glimpse of the pottery-making process. Ask permission before taking photos, though most shops will likely give permission. If a vendor invites you to try out the pottery wheel or help you make something, there will almost always be an expectation that you buy something in return.

Travelers can reach Bat Trang independently by taxi, bus, or hired vehicle. Bus 47 departs every half-hour from the large bus stop near Long Bien Bridge just north of the Old Quarter off Hang Dau street. Cyclists and motorbikes can reach the area by way of Provincial Road 195 on the eastern bank of the river. When crossing, cyclists should use Long Bien Bridge, while other vehicles should use Chuong Duong Bridge directly south.

Van Phuc

West out of town en route to Perfume Pagoda, the whirring looms of **Van Phuc** silk village draw droves of curious shoppers exploring the countryside for the day. As early as the 9th century, local residents raised mulberry trees and silkworms here, spinning their fragile cocoons into fabric for sale both in the village and across the country. During the days of the Nguyen dynasty, Van Phuc was required to produce bolts of silk to clothe the royal family. Today, the village houses over a thousand looms and its goods are often exported beyond Vietnam's borders. While shoppers will find the cost of raw material about the same as in the city, ready-made items like scarves, ties, and shirts are notably less expensive here.

making a clay pot in Bat Trang

Shops generally open at 8am or 9am and close at 5pm daily. Most of the shops in Van Phuc are also workshops. The silk is made there, so you can watch as local proprietors weave different fabrics with a loom. Shop owners are often happy to let you try out the loom, but you will be strongly encouraged to buy something in return.

While most visitors to Van Phuc get here by way of a day tour to Perfume Pagoda, it is also possible to reach Van Phuc independently. Buses 1 and 2 travel out to the village by way of Highway 6, departing from the French Quarter and the lower part of Hoan Kiem district near the train station. Drivers can access Van Phuc via the same route.

Sapa

Perched high above Muong Hoa Valley, the sleepy little town of Sapa is a world apart from its urban contemporaries, quiet and compact amid the vast open space of Vietnam's remote northwest. Now the go-to destination of the region, its rolling hills and verdant, many-tiered rice terraces are the main attraction, coupled with an array of fascinating minority cultures, whose traditional dress, rituals, religious ceremonies, and ways of life continue to exist in much the same fashion as they have for centuries.

Though its tourism industry has seen a boom in recent years, this hilltop town has long captivated visitors, attracting French attention in the early 20th century. Some ethnic Vietnamese moved into the area in the 1960s, but it wasn't until well after the war's end in the 1990s that Sapa saw any major growth spurt.

The fresh air, ample hiking trails, and opportunity for cultural exchange with some of Vietnam's lesser-known communities draw luxury travelers and adventure seekers with the prospect of striking out for minority villages or scaling the colossal Mount Fansipan, Vietnam's tallest peak.

Sapa Lake

Inclement weather can ruin a visit to Sapa. The best months are September and October, just before the rice harvests take away much of its visual appeal, or at the start of spring, for better views of the valley. From November to February, temperatures plummet, earning Sapa a reputation as one of the only towns in Vietnam that sees snow. In winter, heavy fog makes for poor visibility, spoiling much of the point of a visit to Sapa.

SIGHTS

Sapa town is a peaceful, charming little place, meandering across hillsides and dotted with modest green spaces amid its ever-growing town center. All of its sights are easily accessed on foot, though you'll get a workout traipsing up and down some of the nearby inclines. In the town center, a small park dominated by a monument to Ho Chi Minh leads onto the large local square, a popular gathering place in the mornings and evenings. Farther north near the main highway, **Sapa Lake** makes for a pleasant stroll, surrounded by manicured gardens and plenty of park benches.

Sapa Market

Nestled in the hillside just below Sapa's main square, the **central market** (between Fansipan and Cau May streets, 6am-6pm daily) is in full swing from dawn to dusk, alive with vendors hawking bulk items like tea and dried fruit along with fresh produce, meat, and hot meals. A handful of souvenirs and other knickknacks make an appearance, but the stalls set up beneath this market's tented covering stick to the bright and colorful necessities of locals. Even if you're not interested in shopping, it's a pleasant place to wander, as you'll find several items, from greens to tea to fruits that are unique to northwestern Vietnam.

Sapa Museum

Located in a traditional wooden stilt house behind the Tourist Information Center, **Sapa Museum** (2 Fansipan, tel. 02/0387-1975, 7:30am-11:30am and 1:30pm-5pm daily, free) gives a solid introduction to the town and the area, telling the story of Sapa's history under the French and its growth as a town during the 20th century. While a handful of the traditions and customs of Sapa's ethnic minorities are touched upon, there's far less background on the H'mong, Dao, Tay, Phu La, and Giay people who inhabit the region. For this, link up with a local guide to learn more about life in the village.

Our Lady of Rosary Church

The diminutive stone **Our Lady of Rosary Church** (Sapa Town Square, tel. 02/0387-3014, www.sapachurch.org) was first built in 1926 to accommodate Sapa's European parishioners. It is a pretty landmark in town, its gray exterior rounding out the eastern edge of the town square. While the doors are closed outside of mass hours, its steps are often used as a gathering place along with the square nearby.

Sapa

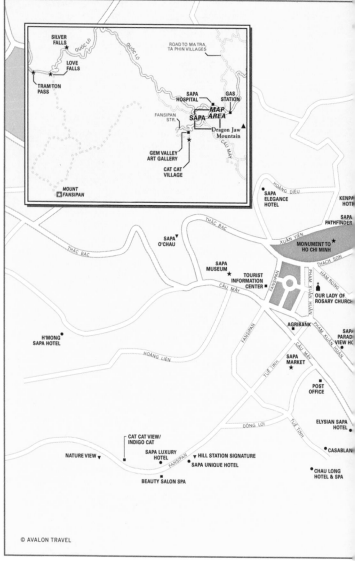

Cat Cat Village

Cat Cat Village (6am-9pm daily, VND50,000) is home to the Black H'mong. The trip to the village is one of the more accessible walks in the Sapa area. This particular jaunt falls somewhere between a hike and a trek (just over three miles round-trip), with paved, well-trodden paths winding through

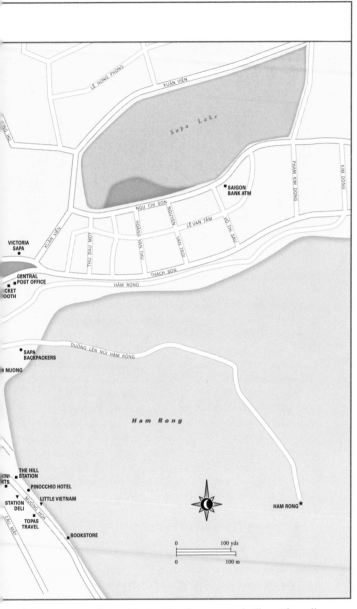

what is now more of a tourist attraction than an actual village. The walk down to Cat Cat from Sapa affords stunning panoramas of Muong Hoa Valley. En route to Cat Cat's ticket booth, you'll pass by small clapboard houses, which remain the most authentic part of the village. Once you've paid and passed through the entry gate, the line of handicraft stalls runs

Our Lady of Rosary Church

almost unbroken from the top of the steps all the way down to Tien Sa Falls, showcasing skirts and scarves, T-shirts, hats, jewelry, and heavily detailed indigo-dyed blankets. Across a suspension bridge that teeters above a rushing waterfall, Black H'mong cultural performances (9am-4pm daily with a break for lunch, additional fee), featuring songs and traditional dances, take place nearly every hour.

Complete the Cat Cat loop by continuing along the stone path and back up. *Xe om* drivers wait just beyond the second bridge and are happy to ferry passengers back to Sapa town (for no more than VND40,000).

For shoppers, it pays to visit when Cat Cat is in full swing (10am-2pm), but travelers who simply want to explore the village and get a glimpse of local life should start by 9am. This early in the day, fewer vendors have set up along the path and you're more likely to elude the roving groups of Black H'mong saleswomen along Fansipan Road. For particularly good views, a bit of local art, and a refreshment, the back veranda of **Gem Valley Art Gallery** (Cat Cat, tel. 09/1284-9753, 7am-10pm daily, VND25,000-100,000) is a fine spot to rest your legs.

Allow yourself 45-60 minutes to complete the trip there and back.

★ Minority Villages

Beyond Sapa's borders, the surrounding hills and valleys are studded with **minority villages** (VND30,000-75,000), particularly those of the Black H'mong and Red Dao. Most of these remote areas bear a resemblance to each other, partly because many groups have coexisted for many years. Visiting any of the minority villages affords visitors a window into the daily lives of Sapa's minority communities, as well as the pleasure of trekking through the verdant landscape. Wander past rows of modest wooden houses, where women dye indigo cloth or embroider intricate designs.

Share a meal with a local family, or even spend the night. Here, several thousand feet above sea level, Sapa's nearby residents are a world apart from the rest of the country.

Just beyond Cat Cat, the next-nearest village, **Sin Chai,** belongs to the Black H'mong and prides itself on its traditional music. The villages of **Ma Tra** and **Ta Phin** to the north, patchwork settlements of Red Dao and Black H'mong households, make equally popular day trips (although locals may be more aggressive with sales pitches in these spots).

Farther south, **Ta Van** is home to a Giay community not far from **Lao Chai** village, another Black H'mong settlement, both of which are popular options and can be visited in a single day. Just beyond these two villages is a Red Dao community, **Giang Ta Chai,** which can also be tacked onto a trek if you're up for the walk. To the east, **Hau Thao, Sa Seng,** and **Hang Da,** all Black H'mong villages, are another worthy option for trekkers.

You'll find useful maps of Sapa's vicinity at the **local tourism office** (2 Fansipan, tel. 02/0387-1975, www.sapa-tourism.com, 8am-5pm daily), which can help you to get the lay of the land.

Hiring a guide (VND200,000-300,000) is a must for these excursions, as you're far more likely to get off the beaten path with a local on hand, and these individuals will have answers for your questions regarding the ins and outs of Sapa's minority cultures. Depending on where you go, a good guide can also help to dissuade villagers from pummeling you with sales pitches. Companies like **ETHOS** (79 Nguyen Chi Thanh, tel. 016/6689-2536, www. ethosspirit.com, 8am-11am and 1:30pm-6pm daily) and **Sapa O'Chau** (8 Thac Bac, tel. 02/0377-1166, www.sapaochau.org, 6:30am-10pm daily) run regular tours to several minority villages. On a tour, travelers hike out to the villages and are bused back to Sapa. The walking distance varies based on which villages are visited, ranging 2.5-10 miles. Tours cover no more than three villages in a day, with most going to only one or two (allowing travelers more time in each village).

Many villages can also be accessed by *xe om,* but this takes most of the fun out of the experience, as Sapa's more secluded landscapes are best explored on foot. All villages in the area charge a VND20,000 entry fee for visitors. Homestays and overnight excursions covering several nearby communities can be arranged (with a tour outfitter or freelance guide).

Silver Falls and Love Falls

Just over six miles out of town, a pair of waterfalls lines the highway up to Tram Ton Pass. The nearest and most popular is **Silver Falls (Thac Bac)** (6am-6pm daily, VND20,000), a charming natural sight. It's not worth the walk up to the top, as you can get the gist from the ground. The walk up is a steep set of stairs, but the going is easy.

Farther up the road, **Love Falls (Thac Tinh Yeu)** (6am-6pm daily, VND50,000) makes more of an impression. Though it's hidden off the highway about a half-mile into the forest, the trek to the falls makes a nice nature walk, strolling through the trees beside Golden Stream (Suoi Vang).

Finding a Guide in Sapa

Budget travelers might find Sapa's tour outfitters out of their price range. The next-best option is to hire an independent local guide in town. While this is decidedly less expensive, it requires extra work, as you'll find many women around Sapa offering to act as guides though few, if any, are certified. On many occasions, a trek with an independent guide turns into a shopping trip, with dozens of handicraft vendors persuading you to part ways with your money.

Recommendations for good local guides can be obtained from your hotel. For extra assurance, spend some time with your guide beforehand. Ask for details about the trip and make your expectations clear—whether you'd prefer an easy hike or a strenuous one, how far you're comfortable walking, whether you're looking to shop or not—prior to setting off.

While it's a greater gamble than booking through a tour outfit, there are independent guides who are great at what they do. Additionally, their entire fee goes directly to them rather than a third party.

You'll need a good pair of shoes and reasonable mobility to reach the end; the stone walkway later deteriorates into a dirt track in some spots, and a few downed trees have crossed the path. The finale, a pretty, moss-covered cascade more than 300 feet tall, makes the journey worthwhile.

Tram Ton Pass

The towering **Tram Ton Pass,** also known as O Quy Ho, is the highest road in Vietnam, coming in at 1.25 miles above sea level. This never-ending maze of switchbacks teeters on the edge of the Hoang Lien mountains, winding its way from Tam Duong, a small town about 30 miles west of Sapa, up along a narrow, cliff-hugging road before plunging back down to Sapa and, later, Lao Cai. While its highest point, perpetually obscured by dense forest, does not afford the kind of awe-inspiring views you might expect, with time and a motorbike (or, for the very fit, a bicycle) you can venture down the serpentine highway, admiring the view from some of its lower sections. Stop at established pullouts to admire the view and take photos. Drivers on this particular road should exercise great caution, as conditions are risky even in good weather and downright treacherous in foul weather. Take extra care when rounding corners and keep a safe distance from the outside shoulder of the road, as it's a straight drop down.

Dragon Jaw Mountain

Rising above Sapa in the southeast, **Dragon Jaw Mountain** (Ham Rong, 7am-7pm daily, VND70,000) affords some pleasant views of town as well as your standard helping of Vietnamese kitsch. The most developed peak in the area, Dragon Jaw bears a spidery network of paths crisscrossing its northern side that look out over the sleepy settlement below as well as toward Fansipan. While it's not exactly a genuine commune with nature, the stone steps that ramble up to the **Cloud Yard,** the platform with the best views of Sapa, are a nice way to pass time on your first day or as you wander around town. Thanks to its paths, solid footwear is not so essential here. You'll want to allow an hour or so to fully explore the winding routes up top. Visitors receive a map of the mountain from the ticket booth; this does little to orient you once you've started on the long stairway up. Regardless, you'll find yourself passing by a restaurant, a rather tired orchid garden, several covered lookouts, a park dotted with statues of the 12 Vietnamese zodiac animals, and, inexplicably, Mickey Mouse.

SIGHTSEEING TOURS

In order to get the most out of exploring Sapa, many travelers sign up for a guided tour to one of the nearby villages, to a bustling local market, or simply deep into the mountains for a homestay. Because so much of Sapa's tourism relies upon connecting with other cultures, it is particularly important to be discerning when choosing a tour company, as you want your experience to be authentic and worthwhile not only on your part but also for the local minorities with whom you interact. There are a handful of trekking and tour outfits in town that focus heavily upon ensuring that the benefits of this region's tourism go directly back to its local residents. If trekking to a nearby minority village is on your itinerary, have a local guide bring you along, as that person will be able to explain the ins and outs of his or her culture better than anyone else.

More than just a trekking outfit, the incredible **Sapa O'Chau** (8 Thac Bac, tel. 02/0377-1166, www.sapaochau.org, 6:30am-10pm daily) does as much for the local community as it does for its customers, providing authentic, adventurous treks off the beaten path as well as changing the lives of Sapa's young ethnic minorities. In a region where many minority children do not attend school beyond adolescence, Shu Tan, a young H'mong woman, has made it her mission to afford local students the

view of Sapa from Dragon Jaw Mountain

skills, education, and opportunities that have long eluded this part of the country. Beginning in 2009 as a single homestay in Lao Chai, the Sapa O'Chau outfit operates a school for local students as well as its tour outfit. Training programs assist aspiring tour guides in gaining experience in the field. Sapa O'Chau is a two-way cultural exchange, in which both travelers and community members benefit. The outfit arranges single-day treks (VND280,000-800,000) and multi-day treks (VND910,000-2,850,000) to various villages in the surrounding area, as well as homestays, market visits, and other adventures. The outfit runs a popular **café** (VND20,000-120,000), which makes some mean fish and chips.

ETHOS (79 Nguyen Chi Thanh, tel. 016/6689-2536, www.ethosspirit. com, 8am-11am and 1:30pm-6pm daily, VND680,000-2,800,000) goes to great lengths to ensure that its tours are not only authentic and far-removed for the tourist crowds but that each of its excursions benefits the local community. From treks into the nearby hillside and village visits that don't appear on any other tour company's itinerary, ETHOS focuses on genuine human interactions with activities like sharing a meal or visiting someone's home that lend themselves more to one-on-one interaction. The tour agency also assists with train bookings and longer trips, including a guided tour of the Northwest Loop.

SHOPPING

As the only major tourist town in the northwest, shopping is a popular activity in Sapa, particularly when the fog rolls in to obscure its panoramic views. The main handicraft of the H'mong and Red Dao is textiles; both groups are equally skilled in colorful and detailed embroidery, which often features on skirts, jackets, blankets, bags, and other accessories. Silver jewelry and indigo-dyed items are another specialty of the H'mong. Along Cau May and Muong Hoa streets, plenty of retailers hawk knockoff North Face items for the Fansipan-bound, while handicrafts are virtually everywhere,

textiles for sale in the Sapa market

including on the arms of roving vendors, whose sales pitches range from friendly to downright aggressive.

Hidden beneath the Cat Cat View Hotel, **Indigo Cat** (46 Fansipan, tel. 09/8240-3647, www.indigocat.asia, 8am-7pm Sun.-Fri.) is a small shop that specializes in Fair Trade products made by H'mong women, namely bracelets, bags, skirts, jewelry, and a few other odds and ends. Look out for the small handouts scattered throughout the store, which explain the significance of many of the intricate patterns you see swirled and looped and stitched across the clothing of local minority women. Indigo Cat also sells pre-packaged DIY sewing kits so that you can make your own H'mong-style bracelet using traditional embroidery patterns. Swing by in the afternoons and one of the shop's owners, a H'mong woman, will help to get you started on the craft with an impromptu sewing class.

The town's only **bookstore** (Muong Hoa, 8am-7pm daily) hides a short walk down Muong Hoa on the left-hand side. Stocked with photocopied paperbacks and a few genuine books, the shop's titles include old and new English-language favorites. Prices aren't listed, so feel free to haggle, particularly if you purchase more than one item.

SPORTS AND RECREATION

With plenty of green space, rolling hills, and incredible scenery, Sapa is an active destination. Sapa is the home base for trekking day trips to surrounding villages and overnight homestays with local families. These journeys range from leisurely to challenging, with Mount Fansipan being the mother of all treks, but there's also room for cycling and, when the weather takes a turn, a hard-earned massage.

Trekking

With dozens of small communities peppering the mountains and valleys of northwestern Vietnam, gaining access to the more authentic, untouched villages of the area requires at least some travel on foot up the steep inclines of the surrounding hills and along the muddy dirt paths that lead to Sapa's more remote residences. In town, easier walks to **Cat Cat Village** and around **Dragon Jaw Mountain** are blessed with paved roads and stone steps. Once you leave town the highway branches off into smaller, rockier trails that bring you away from the buzz of Sapa's tourist center and out to peaceful paddies and stunning mountain vistas. For standard day-long treks and one-night homestays, bring along water and a sturdy pair of shoes. For longer excursions, especially to Fansipan, you'll need to stock up on proper trekking gear. Scores of shops in the area sell North Face goods, most of them knockoffs but some genuine, as well as a host of hiking boots, first-aid essentials, and the like.

Two companies that provide guided treks are **Sapa O'Chau** (8 Thac Bac, tel. 02/0377-1166, www.sapaochau.org, 6:30am-10pm daily) and **ETHOS** (79 Nguyen Chi Thanh, tel. 016/6689-2536, www.ethosspirit.com, 8am-11am and 1:30pm-6pm daily).

Exploring the Northwest Loop

Venture into Vietnam's far north and you'll discover another world altogether, awash with rich green rice paddies and wide, flowing rivers that wind around the region's many oversized landscapes. Those who strike out on Vietnam's **Northwest Loop** will be handsomely rewarded with soaring mountains, plunging valleys, isolated villages, and unfathomable vistas. This is an independent adventure on which you'll find few to no English speakers, no high-end hotels, and not a Western meal to speak of. The views from the northwest's serpentine roads make it well worth the journey.

Starting from Hanoi, this 720-mile circuit runs west toward Dien Bien Phu, the city where Vietnam defeated its French enemies once and for all, turning north past Muong Lay and Lai Chau, before scaling the death-defying cliffs of Tram Ton Pass, rolling into Sapa town, and coasting back down to the capital.

Most travelers make the trip on a motorbike in about a week; cyclists can complete the Northwest Loop in two weeks. Invest in a quality vehicle for the journey, as there aren't many repair shops in the area. What shops do exist have far more experience with motorbikes than multi-speed bicycles. Cyclists should stock up on tools, tubes, and other necessities before leaving Hanoi. Before you set off, commit the Vietnamese words for hotel (*khach san*, pronounced "cack san"), guesthouse (*nha nghi*, pronounced "nyah ngee"), and restaurant (*nha hang*, pronounced "nyah hang") to memory, as these will be essential when you're looking for a place to stop.

Road conditions throughout this region are good, with smooth, sleek asphalt most of the way. Opt for heavy-duty tires on both bicycles and motorbikes. Guardrails and barriers are nonexistent. Even though there's little traffic on the roads of the northwest, serious accidents can happen and adequate medical care is a long way away.

A handful of tour outfits in Sapa arrange guided, Easy Rider-style motorbike tours that follow this route, though the cost will be astronomically greater than doing it on your own. You can usually arrange these tours in Hanoi or Sapa and expect to take at least six days to complete the full circuit.

★ MOUNT FANSIPAN

Towering above its surroundings, **Mount Fansipan** is often referred to as the "Roof of Indochina," standing well above any other peak in neighboring Laos or Cambodia. Looming over the opposite flank of the Muong Hoa Valley, its silhouette can be seen from the town's hillside windows on a clear day and has begun to attract a growing number of ambitious travelers hoping to reach the summit. Though its trails are a little worse for wear, cluttered with rubbish and beginning to get too well-worn for some, the enigmatic mountain remains a point of interest among many adventure-seeking tourists.

Guided excursions to the top can be attempted in as little as a day or as long as 3-5 days, depending upon your level of fitness and your willingness to sleep in the rather damp and dingy camps that hover around 7,000 and 9,000 feet. One-day treks up to the summit are not for the faint of heart: It's a 10-hour hike at best and the gently rolling trails at the start of the journey soon give way to steeper climbs and a final push up to the summit. Instead, reasonably fit travelers may want to opt for a two-day trip, while those who'd prefer to take their time can venture out into the wild for longer. Shrouded in a bluish haze, the view from 10,311 feet can be fickle even during the summer months, as wind, rain, and other elements have a mind of their own up here. Standing next to the pyramidal marker that signals the end of your uphill climb is well worth the wet shoes and chilly temperatures.

Climbers who sign up for a trip to the top should invest in a sturdy pair of hiking boots and some warm clothes. A decent jacket is still recommended in summer, as the air cools down significantly at this height. Most guided tours begin around VND1,050,000 per person for a single-day excursion, including transportation, entry fees, a guide, and, for overnight trips, a porter or two. When booking your Fansipan trek, it's important to be clear about what's included in the tour, as you'll want to know whether things like water and snacks are provided or you should be packing your own.

It's highly advised that you pay for the necessary guide for this trek. Going it alone is not only forbidden, but could easily become dangerous. In 2016, a young British hiker went missing during an unguided Fansipan trek and was later found dead. There is little to direct you once you set out for the summit and, particularly in foul weather, the trail becomes a treacherous, rain-soaked path.

If you're really not up for the physical challenge, a **cable car** (tel. 02/0381-8888, www.fansipanlegend.com.vn, 7:30am-5:30pm daily, VND600,000 round-trip, VND400,000 for children) makes the trip up to Fansipan's peak as well. While the 6,292.5-meter system managed to break two Guinness

Mount Fansipan, the "Roof of Indochina"

World Records (longest nonstop three-rope cable car and greatest elevation difference by a nonstop three-rope cable car), its presence has taken a bit of the magic out of scaling the Roof of Indochina. Cable cars depart from a station located between Cat Cat and Sin Chai villages.

Cycling

There are a small number of local companies that arrange cycling tours or rent mountain bikes to individuals. These excursions are expensive, a fact justified by the quality of the equipment, but then take all the challenge out of the trip by driving travelers uphill before allowing them to roll down to the bottom. Some companies offer customized tours.

To combine cycling with a bit of sightseeing, rent a mountain bike and blaze your own trail up to Silver Falls and Tram Ton Pass. For more in-depth excursions, book a tour, as the area is remote and finding your way can be difficult without someone to guide you.

Two companies providing bike tours of the area are **Sapa Pathfinder** (13 Xuan Vien, tel. 02/0387-3468, www.sapapathfinder.com, 7:30am-7pm daily) and **ETHOS** (79 Nguyen Chi Thanh, tel. 016/6689-2536, www.ethosspirit.com, 8am-11am and 1:30pm-6pm daily). Sapa Pathfinder rents out well-maintained Trek mountain bikes (VND225,000/day).

Massages and Spas

When the fog rolls into Sapa and a heavy mist obscures its picture-perfect views, a popular activity among weary travelers is a trip to the spa. While there are several outfits in town that advertise spa services, including a traditional Red Dao herbal bath, these are hit or miss. For assured quality at a higher price, the spa at **Victoria Sapa** (Xuan Vien, tel. 02/0387-1522, www.victoriahotels.asia, 8am-10pm daily, VND630,000-1,260,000) provides massage services and other treatments. Non-guests are welcome to visit Victoria's sauna or pool (VND210,000 pp). For a more affordable option, the **Beauty Salon Spa** (43 Fansipan, tel. 09/7789-3566, 9am-11pm daily, VND120,000-300,000) opposite Sapa Luxury Hotel does a decent job, with quality spa services.

FOOD

You won't find too many regional dishes in this foggy northern town, but local favorites include miniature barbecue skewers, which make for an excellent afternoon snack, as well as roast suckling pig, which you'll find on a spit in front of a few eateries in town. Though it's not native to the area, trout has become a popular local commodity. Sapa's minority groups also have some dishes of their own. Most restaurants in town seem to hold to the notion that Western travelers would prefer Western food, and so it can be tricky to find more authentic Vietnamese fare, though one or two restaurants in Sapa town excel at providing genuine homemade meals. For cheaper options, stick to the market stalls, as Sapa's eateries, almost all of which cater to foreign tourists, come at a price.

Learn to Cook the Sapa Way

The Hill Station Signature restaurant (37 Fansipan, tel. 02/0388-7111, www.thehillstation.com) runs a **H'mong cooking class** (VND750,000) for culinary-minded travelers. During the class, you'll visit a local market to pick out ingredients, work with an English-speaking chef, and learn how to create a menu of five H'mong dishes. Students also visit a farm in nearby Hau Thao village, run by a local family, where the restaurant gets all of its ingredients.

Clustered around the foot of Dragon Jaw Mountain beneath a maze of tarpaulins are several *do nuong* (barbecue) vendors (mid-morning-late afternoon daily, VND5,000-10,000/skewer). These tiny stalls are no more than a single miniature grill and a few tables. The colorful displays of skewers, packed with everything from pork and veggies to chicken wings, dumplings, and tofu, are enticing after a long walk up the mountain. Often accompanied by bamboo tubes of sticky rice, these tasty morsels are enjoyed as a snack or alongside a few drinks and hit the spot during cold, rainy weather.

A local restaurant, **Co Lich** (1 Fansipan, tel. 09/1282-8260, 7:30am-midnight daily, VND60,000-300,000), at the top of Fansipan street, does a tasty suckling pig, which appears on the rotating spit out front. Beyond pork, you'll find a slew of Vietnamese meat and vegetable dishes on its extensive menu, all at reasonable prices.

Though it's nearly invisible from outside, tucked soundly beneath the Sapa Paradise View Hotel is its restaurant, **Paradise View Restaurant** (Sapa Paradise View Hotel, 18 Pham Xuan Huan, tel. 02/0387-2683, www.sapaparadiseviewhotel.com, 6:30am-9pm daily, VND50,000-150,000), a cozy little spot that prides itself on serving only top-notch barbecue and hotpot dishes. Diners in the mood for authentic local fare will appreciate the restaurant's select offerings, namely the mouthwatering salmon hotpot, whose ingredients are picked fresh from a tank at the back of the restaurant, not to mention the cheerful and conscientious staff.

The charming **Little Sapa** (18 Cau May, tel. 02/0387-1222, 8am-9pm daily, VND45,000-150,000) may well be one of the most affordable eateries in a town of tourist-heavy restaurants. Its well-rounded menu of Vietnamese dishes showcase a more genuine version of Vietnamese cuisine and, while Little Sapa's clientele is largely foreign, the prices and tastes are more local than its competition. Indoors, embroidered tablecloths and plenty of festive lighting add some cheer, and the staff are an industrious and friendly bunch.

Little Vietnam (33 Muong Hoa, 8:30am-last customer daily, VND45,000-200,000) operates out of a tiny, cozy wooden storefront along Muong Hoa just opposite the Bamboo Sapa Hotel. Vietnamese cuisine takes up most of the menu, offering more than just your standard backpacker fare, with a few burgers and sandwiches rounding out the list. Staff are friendly, and most prices manage to come in under VND100,000, making this one of the more affordable spots in the tourist area.

Perched on the hillside overlooking Muong Hoa Valley, **Nature View** (51 Fansipan, tel. 02/0387-1438, 8am-10pm daily, VND60,000-150,000) boasts some of the best views in town, not to mention an extensive list of Vietnamese fare, including chicken, beef, pork, fish, duck, deer, and wild boar. An especially tasty vegetarian set menu is also on offer for lunch and dinner. Regardless of whether you come for a full-blown meal or just an afternoon drink, the breathtaking panoramas from Nature View's dining room are what set the place apart, with large windows and an open-air rooftop affording a clear sight to the valley below.

The chic and omnipresent **Hill Station** (7 Muong Hoa, tel. 02/0388-7111, www.thehillstation.com, 7:30am-10:30pm daily, VND75,000-275,000) is clearly doing well for itself, as the trendy eatery now counts a deli, boutique, and signature Vietnamese restaurant in its offerings around town. At its main venue, an exposed brick building just near the foot of Cau May, you'll find deli-style sandwiches, pastries, cheese, and charcuterie on the menu, while the small black-and-white boutique down the road stocks jars of Sapa honey, tea, genuine H'mong jewelry, and other souvenirs.

For an upscale and authentic meal, the ★ **Hill Station Signature** (37 Fansipan, tel. 02/0388-7111, www.thehillstation.com, 7:30am-10:30pm daily, VND70,000-145,000) showcases a host of dishes unique to Sapa's minority cultures, from banana flower salad to fried chicken with wild ginger and smoked pork belly. Vegetarian options are available, taking advantage of several mountain greens you won't find elsewhere in Vietnam, along with homemade tofu. Throw in a bit of rustic chic, with low tables and mounds of hemp as seat cushions, simple porcelain, and a killer view of the valley, and Hill Station Signature is easily one of the best eateries in town. Higher tables are also available.

Hill Station Signature

ACCOMMODATIONS

You'll find plenty of excellent mid-range and luxury accommodations lining the two main tourist streets of town, Cau May and Fansipan, not to mention a scattering of other hotels that ramble up the nearby hillside, affording incredible views of Muong Hoa Valley. Thanks to some fierce competition in the area, travelers can look forward to well-appointed rooms, plush furnishings, and a higher level of service in most hotels above the VND525,000 mark. Solo travelers and those on a shoestring are not spoiled for choice. A handful of quality budget hotels offer well-kept rooms at good prices; dorm beds are few and far between, especially if your requirements include clean bedding and bathrooms. A small number of dorm accommodations exist, namely in the budget hotels along Fansipan street.

SAPA

Under VND210,000

Dorm beds at the **Southern Sapa Hotel** (33 Fansipan, tel. 02/0350-2633, www.phuongnamhotelsapa.com, VND250,000-1,500,000) are some of the most generous in Vietnam, offering a queen-size mattress to weary travelers, along with bright and spacious rooms. En suite bathrooms are small but clean and the back door leads onto a tiny ledge with stunning views of the valley. Hot water and air-conditioning are included.

VND210,000-525,000

Amid the jumble of shops and restaurants along Cau May, **Elysian Sapa Hotel** (38 Cau May, tel. 02/0387-1238, www.elysiansapahotel.com, VND385,000-1,270,000) represents a solid budget option, with cozy beds, hot water, air-conditioning, TV, Wi-Fi, and tea- and coffee-making facilities in each room. Electric blankets and other accoutrements are available during the winter months. Downstairs, the hotel runs a restaurant as well as a travel desk and assists with tour arrangements.

The friendly folks at **Casablanca** (26 Dong Loi, tel. 02/0387-2667, VND360,000-680,000) offer decent guest rooms with standard amenities such as air-conditioning, hot water, TV, Wi-Fi, and tea- and coffee-making facilities. The staff is especially cheerful and service-minded, and the location, wedged between the larger tourist streets of Cau May and Fansipan, provides a break from the shops and activity nearby. Breakfast is included in the room rate, but it is possible to book accommodations without the additional cost.

VND525,000-1,050,000

Amid the droves of accommodations overlooking the valley, ★ **Sapa Luxury Hotel** (36 Fansipan, tel. 02/0387-2771, www.sapaluxuryhotel.com, VND640,000-2,000,000, breakfast included) stands out for its exceptional hospitality. This family-owned boutique hotel is just a stone's throw from several of the town's main attractions, including Cat Cat Village, the local market, and Cau May shopping street. All rooms are clean and spacious, featuring walk-in showers and twin- or queen-size beds. Rooms are equipped with a mini-bar, television, computer, and Wi-Fi. A complimentary Vietnamese or Western breakfast is served each morning. Depending on the season, it's best to book early, as there are only 10 rooms. The hotel offers pickup service from the train station in Lao Cai for those who call ahead. For budget travelers, small but tidy rooms are available in the back without a mountain view, but for the full experience book a room in the front, where the balcony offers breathtaking panoramas of the valley and Mount Fansipan.

The reason for the success of **Cat Cat View** (46 Fansipan, tel. 02/0387-1946, www.catcathotel.com, VND800,000-1,370,000, breakfast included) is in its name. Rising above the smaller buildings across the street, this hotel boasts some incredible views of the valley and, while its rooms are basic, you'll find hot water, air-conditioning, TV, and Wi-Fi among the hotel's amenities, along with electric blankets for the winter months and additional services, such as DVD players and space heaters, available for rent. Discounts are sometimes available for multi-night stays.

While the **Sapa Unique Hotel** (39 Fansipan, tel. 02/0387-2008, www.sapauniquehotel.com, VND1,480,000-1,925,000) is as good as any on the block, its staff set the place apart with top-notch service and a genuine effort to ensure that travelers enjoy their stay. Rooms are cozy and well-appointed, featuring hot water, air-conditioning, Wi-Fi, television, and modern furnishings. The attached travel outfit, Viet Sapa, is notably reliable.

Tucked off the town's main square, **Sapa Elegance Hotel** (3 Hoang Dieu, tel. 02/0388-8668, www.sapaelegancehotel.com, VND735,000-910,000, breakfast included) earns top marks for its location, overlooking the valley but just far enough removed to lie beyond the reach of Sapa's touristy streets. Outfitted in cozy, modern furnishings, each guest room features hot water, Wi-Fi access, television, a dual air-conditioning and heating system, minibar, in-room safe, and tea- and coffee-making facilities. The hotel's pleasant staff assist with tours and travel arrangements.

Sapa Elegance Hotel

A breathtaking view of the valley and mountains rolling off into the distance win **H'mong Sapa Hotel** (27 Thac Bac, tel. 02/0377-2228, www.hmongsapahotel.com, VND910,000-2,500,000, breakfast included) huge points, complemented nicely by the friendly service, restaurant, mountain view terrace, and excellent tour outfit. Superior accommodations are well-furnished with hot water, TV, Wi-Fi, and an air-conditioning system that blows hot and cold. For a private balcony, upgrade to a deluxe room. Booking directly with the hotel tends to get you a discount.

Perched on the hillside above Cau May, the **Sapa Paradise View** (18 Pham Xuan Huan, tel. 02/0387-2683, www.sapaparadiseviewhotel.com, VND1,025,000-1,935,000, breakfast included) wins top points for service. Rooms are comfortable and well-appointed, with an in-room safe, television, Wi-Fi access, hot water, and an in-room computer. The upper floors afford pleasant views, while certain rooms also include a private balcony. The hotel assists with booking tours and other travel arrangements. Its ground-floor restaurant is a popular choice, with delicious barbecue and hotpot gracing the menu.

Over VND2,100,000

A beautiful, well-hidden resort overlooking this sleepy town, **Victoria Sapa** (Xuan Vien, tel. 02/0387-1522, www.victoriahotels.asia, VND3,490,000-5,515,000) boasts 77 rooms, a private terrace, and stunning views of the surrounding area thanks to its hillside perch. Spacious accommodations include TV, Wi-Fi access, air-conditioning, hot water, and tea- and coffee-making facilities. Superior, deluxe, and suite rooms are available, some of which come with private balconies. The resort counts a top-notch restaurant, bar, spa, fitness center, kids club, tennis court, and indoor heated pool in its offerings.

INFORMATION AND SERVICES

Sapa's **Tourist Information Center** (2 Fansipan, tel. 02/0387-1975, www.sapa-tourism.com, 8am-5pm daily) is one of the more helpful of its kind, dispensing free advice and maps with a smile. Tours can be arranged without the hard sell you might find elsewhere.

The only bank located in the more touristy part of town is an **Agribank** (Cau May, tel. 02/0387-1107, www.agribank.com.vn, 7:30am-11:30am and 1:30pm-5pm Mon.-Fri.) on Cau May, which also has an ATM next door. Should you run into any trouble with this machine, you can find a **Saigon Bank ATM** (corner of Ngu Chi Son and Vo Thi Sau) farther into town, near the lake outside the Riverside II Hotel.

Sapa's **post office** (20 Cau May, tel. 02/0387-1247, 7:30am-noon and 1:30pm-5pm daily) runs a small branch near the market that can handle mail and postal services for travelers. For more in-depth queries, swing by the **central post office** (6 Thach Son, tel. 02/0387-1298, 7am-9pm daily).

The local **hospital** (Dien Bien Phu, tel. 02/0351-8558) sits on the northern edge of town. But, medical care in the remote northern mountains is well below par compared to Vietnamese cities. In the event of an emergency and for any serious issues, head back to Hanoi.

GETTING THERE
By Bus

Buses to Sapa can be tricky to find. **Hung Thanh** (162B Tran Quang Khai, tel. 04/3927-4285, 8am-7pm daily, VND300,000) is a reliable company that runs overnight sleeper buses from Hanoi to Sapa and vice versa. Buses leave from Hanoi at 7am and 10pm daily and arrive right beside Sapa Lake. For the return trip to Hanoi, book your seat through the **ticket booth** (6 Thach Son, 7am-9pm daily) outside Sapa's central post office. There's just one ticket vendor, who may be out when you're there. Phone for someone to sell you the ticket if that happens.

While a handful of bus companies operate buses back to Hanoi, you'll want to be discerning in which one you choose, as the mountain road leading to Sapa is winding and narrow; safe, experienced drivers are an absolute must. Hung Thanh is your best bet above the others.

By Train

When heading to Sapa, the preferred method of travel is by sleeper train. Bare-bones hard sleeper cabins feature a single thin palette accompanied by a worn blanket and pillow. For more comfort, a number of private companies run plush, soft sleepers equipped with air-conditioning, comfier mattresses, and cleaner bedding. A lower berth ticket allows you to be closer to your belongings, which will inevitably be slid underneath the bottom bunk; while it's not especially common, theft does occur on sleeper trains.

Ticket prices among Hanoian travel agents vary drastically based on the agent's fee; ask around before settling on an agency. For the best possible fare, buy your ticket from the train station. Lines and organization are not a major focus at the ticketing counter, but there are one or two agents who speak English and can help to arrange your trip. The journey from Sapa to Hanoi is easier to sort out, with the **ticket booth** (6 Thach Son, 7am-9pm daily) outside the central post office quoting some of the better rates in town. The route back to Hanoi is mysteriously more expensive: where you can find a hard sleeper from Hanoi to Sapa at about VND450,000, you'll be paying at least VND600,000 for the same trip in the opposite direction. The commission attached to train tickets in Sapa runs VND40,000-100,000.

The final stop for northbound trains is not Sapa (which does not have a train station), but the **Lao Cai train station,** roughly 23 miles northeast of town near the Chinese border. From Lao Cai, get to Sapa by taking a minibus. The standard fare for a trip from Lao Cai to Sapa city center is VND50,000. There are enough minibuses around that you can walk away from anyone who attempts to overcharge. Before paying, get confirmation that the tout leading you to a particular minibus is affiliated with that vehicle—with so many people around, it's easy to pay your fare up-front,

Wait until you reach town before handing over the fare.

GETTING AROUND
Taxis and *Xe Om*
Plenty of *xe om* drivers hang out near the town square, waiting to offer a
ride or rent a motorbike to you. For larger vehicles, call a **Fansipan** (tel.
02/0362-6262) taxi. Keep in mind, most everything in Sapa is within walking distance and there are few scenarios in which you'd need to take a cab,
with the exception of Silver Falls.

Vehicles for Hire
Walking around downtown Sapa, you'll see tons of hotels and independent enterprises renting motorbikes to travelers. Semi-automatic vehicles
run around VND80,000 per day, while an automatic will set you back
VND100,000 a day. Check the brakes and all other functions of the bike
before taking off, as roads are steep and medical attention is far away. While
traffic may move slower on the uphills, many a truck or motorbike will
come racing down an incline at top speed, not always on the appropriate
side of the road, and locals often walk along the shoulder of the highway.

Background

The Landscape

Covering a total area of 127,880 square miles, Vietnam is a skinny, S-shaped country that snakes its way from the southern border of China all the way down to the mouth of the mighty Mekong. While there is no official nickname for the country, its shape is sometimes likened to a dragon, a moniker which locals are happy to accept, as this mythical creature has ties to the origin story of the Vietnamese people. To the west, Vietnam shares a frontier with both Cambodia and Laos, while the north is bordered by China. Along the southern and eastern edges of the country is the East Sea, also known as the South China Sea.

GEOGRAPHY

While Vietnam's rice paddies seem to go on for miles across the Mekong and Red River Deltas, only about 20 percent of the country's land area is actually flat. The rest of Vietnam, from low, rolling hills along the southern coast to the soaring peaks of the far north, spans a range of elevations. Near the sea, white-sand beaches are dotted with clusters of tropical foliage. The dense jungle of Vietnam's mountainous regions, including the Central Highlands and much of the area north of Hanoi, is all but impenetrable.

Down south, the low-lying Mekong Delta is an unusual combination of water and land. This is largely a result of the region's namesake river, a mammoth waterway that begins in eastern Tibet and flows through several Southeast Asian nations before splintering into nine separate tributaries across the Vietnamese border. Moving along the coast, the shores east of Ho Chi Minh City bear an odd climate that lends itself to a coupling of tropical beaches and barren sand dunes. The country's interior is comprised of undulating mountains and lush jungle that extend all the way to the western border. Up north, the Red River Delta creates a similar effect to its southern counterpart, with an expanse of pancake-flat rice paddies around Hanoi extending toward the coast, punctuated only by limestone karsts, the same rocky outcroppings you'll see in Ha Long Bay and around Phong Nha-Ke Bang National Park, which rise unexpectedly out of these level landscapes. Along the northern border, the terrain becomes mountainous once again, rising and falling dramatically all the way from the East Sea west through Ha Giang and Lao Cai provinces to Laos. This region is also home to Vietnam's highest peak, Mount Fansipan (10,311 ft.).

CLIMATE

While the majority of Vietnam never really gets cold, the northern and southern halves of the country experience two very different weather patterns. Residents in Hanoi and the surrounding region see four seasons

---

Previous: a lotus, the national flower of Vietnam; water puppets for sale in the Old Quarter.

throughout the year, though they are not as distinct as North American seasons. Up north, a cold, damp winter and a sweltering hot summer are separated by a few months of mild weather on either side. Temperatures in this part of the country fluctuate from a brisk 50°F in January to 100°F in July and August. Pack warm clothes if you plan to visit in winter, as Hanoi does not have heaters and the bone-chilling humidity can be deceptive. In the extreme north, some areas along the border even experience snow, though this is never more than a light dusting on mountain peaks and rooftops.

In the southern and central regions, temperatures remain more consistent, varying only a few degrees between the rainy and dry seasons. Rainy season begins when temperatures are highest, breaking the heat with heavy rainfall for a few hours each day. These rains remain consistent until the end of the season, at which time a constant downpour ushers in slightly cooler weather. Dry season still sees some precipitation, though significantly less, as well as lower temperatures and occasional winds, with the heat building over time until rainy season returns. Depending upon your location, these seasons come at different times of year, with the rains arriving in May down south and ending in late October, while the central region experiences rainy season from September to January. For southern Vietnam, temperatures usually change no more than a few degrees, holding steady around 90°F, with varying levels of humidity depending upon the season. While central Vietnam's climate is more similar to the south than the north, this region experiences a wider range of temperatures, from a cool 65°F to around 85°F in the summer, as well as more intense storms. Danang, central Vietnam's most cosmopolitan city, is also the mainland's easternmost point. As a result, the surrounding area experiences yearly typhoons, which bring heavy rainfall and high winds, which have been known to destroy homes and farmland near the coast.

ENVIRONMENTAL ISSUES

Vietnam has a poor track record on both conservation and clean-up efforts. A handful of NGOs and other independent organizations do their part to help protect the country's natural resources. Despite enacting laws to safeguard its forests and waterways, environmental regulations are only sometimes enforced to protect the country's natural resources, leading to issues such as water shortages and deforestation. In the Central Highlands, scores of hydropower plants harness the strength of the region's rivers for economic benefit, but the dams that come with these facilities often dry up riverbeds below, eliminating a valuable water source for downstream communities.

Industrial pollution has become a hot-button issue in recent years. In April 2016, a Taiwanese steel company dumped large amounts of toxic wastewater into the East Sea, killing an estimated 70 tons of fish and other marine life along a 124-mile stretch of central Vietnam's coast. The mass fish death affected the region's many fishermen and brought the country's seafood industry to a grinding halt. Though this incident was the largest and most publicized case, smaller instances of industrial pollution continue to take place elsewhere in the country, affecting local waterways and the people who rely on them to survive.

Along the coast, specifically in urban areas, air pollution is also a growing problem. Though Vietnamese cities are not as bad as some of their East Asian counterparts, rapid industrialization and expanding metropolitan areas are cause for future concern as nearby suburbs are devoured by modern development and increased pollution from traffic and factories leaves air quality diminished.

While none of the urban rivers, canals, or lakes you see may look like a nice place for a swim, officials in cities like HCMC and Hanoi have done a tremendous amount of work to rehabilitate these heavily polluted waterways. Garbage collection takes place on a daily basis and younger generations are more conscious of how their individual actions can affect Vietnam's urban pollution.

Beyond these issues, the country's greatest challenge is bringing attention to the value of its natural resources and encouraging its citizens to clean up. More than a few breathtaking landscapes in Vietnam are clouded by reckless littering. While urban centers employ hundreds of street cleaners to remedy this, rural areas and smaller towns are often left to languish in their own garbage, and there is a general expectation that someone else will clean up a person's litter.

Plants and Animals

Stretching over 2,000 miles along the East Sea, Vietnam is home to countless varieties of flora and fauna. From the peaks of Sapa all the way down to the watery Mekong Delta, the country's range of climates and habitats lends itself to an equally diverse array of plant and wildlife. However, with an ever-growing population and a rapid pace of development, many of Vietnam's plant and animal species are in danger. Deforestation and the overuse of natural resources threaten to erase natural habitats, while several species, some of which are unique to Vietnam, have become critically endangered in recent years due to the illegal wildlife trade. Today, Vietnam is home to nine "death row" species, or critically endangered animals endemic to Vietnam, according to the International Union for Conservation of Nature (IUCN). High demand for animal parts, such as rhino horn, has also forced a handful of primates, turtles, and other creatures onto the IUCN Red List, which documents the world's most endangered flora and fauna. Vietnam is the leading market for the illegal rhino horn trade.

While Vietnam boasts 30 protected national parks, not all are strictly supervised. Authorities have stepped up their punishment of poachers in recent years, but the wildlife trade continues to be a problem in Vietnam. In 2011, WWF confirmed that the country's small population of Javan rhino, an extremely rare animal, was officially extinct after the last of its kind was likely killed by poachers. Additionally, nearly one-third of the country's protected lands are in and around the Mekong Delta, a region already straining under high population density. While the forests and jungles of Vietnam contain countless fascinating creatures, the country still has a ways to go in protecting its natural resources and bringing the 77 species of flora and fauna currently listed as critically endangered on IUCN's Red List back to a healthy number.

PLANTS

According to the World Bank's World Development Indicators, over 45 percent of Vietnam's land area is covered by forest. These woodlands can be broken down into several categories, from the dry lowland forests of southern Vietnam, largely made up of tropical hardwood, to the flooded forests of mangroves and cajuput trees in that same region. Highland forests cover the northern region under a dense canopy of broad-leaved trees and moss. Inland, cooler climates like that of Lang Biang Plateau, are home to pine forests, which coexist alongside groves of bamboo. Fruit trees are common in the Mekong Delta, with jackfruit, durian, longans, rambutans, and papayas aplenty. Commercially prized woods like teak, rosewood, and ebony are raised here, as is bamboo. Rattan, an extremely durable wood used in basket-weaving, particularly by the minority communities of the north, is also prevalent.

ANIMALS

A growing number of people are flocking to the country's seaside areas, pushing many animals out of their natural habitats. In a region with many endemic species, Vietnam's fauna holds its own array of endangered creatures. Larger species like the Indochinese tiger, moon bear, and Asian elephant often take center stage thanks to their size and prominence around the world, but Vietnam is also home to a host of native species that are found only within its borders. Even today, scientists continue to discover rare creatures, like the thorny tree frog, an amphibian that lives only among the highest peaks of Vietnam in its remote northern region, and as late as the 1990s, large mammals were still being found in the dense forests of central and northern Vietnam. The most elusive of these is the saola, an ox-like creature with long horns that is sometimes called the Asian unicorn due to its rarity.

Chances are you won't get a glimpse of Vietnam's more exotic animals during your visit. Travelers are more likely to encounter domestic creatures during their trip: chickens are common even in urban centers like Ho Chi Minh City, where they are sometimes kept as pets; pigs and water buffalo are abundant in the countryside.

Those eager to see Vietnam's more exotic creatures, particularly its many varieties of primates, are encouraged to view these animals in the wild rather than at a zoo or tourist attraction, as the creatures in these centers tend to be mistreated and sometimes aggressive. The majority of Vietnam's wildlife lives in national parks and nature reserves. National parks in Con Dao and Cat Ba have wild populations of different primates, including macaques, langurs, and gibbons, while both Cuc Phuong National Park and the Cu Chi Wildlife Rescue Center rehabilitate endangered primates, turtles, and other animals captured in the wildlife trade, providing a closer look at these creatures in an environment where they are safe and well looked after.

Mammals

While, in name, Vietnam continues to boast incredible biodiversity, today many of its mammal species exist only in protected wildlife areas. Fast-paced development and growing populations have encroached upon the natural habitats of many species, including the country's array of primate species. Macaques are far and away the most common and can be found in national parks and nature reserves from north to south. Endemic species like the Cat Ba, Ha Tinh, and douc langurs, also found in government-protected forests, are trickier to spot given their smaller numbers. Still, there's a chance you might catch a glimpse of these creatures in their respective habitats. Beyond primates, Vietnam's mammals include Asiatic black bears, banteng, gaur, deer, pangolins, and dugongs.

Reptiles and Amphibians

Reptiles are one of Vietnam's more visible categories of fauna, and you're likely to spot a few geckos on the walls, even in urban areas. Several species of turtle, a revered animal in Vietnamese lore, exist throughout the country, from the massive Yangtze softshell turtle, of which just one remains in Vietnam, to several smaller varieties, such as the Chinese three-striped box turtle and the Indochinese box turtle, both of which appear on Vietnam's endangered species list. While the future of these animals is precarious, new species are still being discovered in some of Vietnam's more remote areas. As recently as 2014, scientists came upon a previously unknown variety of tree frog living in the mountainous central region. Along the coast, snakes are equally elusive thanks to the country's growing population. There are over 200 different varieties of snakes in Vietnam, including 60 venomous species, many of which appear in the wilder interior regions.

Birds

Vietnam's wealth of feathered friends are a birder's dream. Over 850 different varieties of bird live within the country's borders, including the highest number of endemic species in mainland Southeast Asia. The rarest of these is the Edwards' pheasant, among the most endangered species in the world. There are also several varieties of laughingthrush that are endangered. Southern Vietnam, namely the Mekong Delta, is a prime location to catch a glimpse of the country's array of bird species. With endless flooded fields and high trees, sanctuaries such as Tra Su and Tram Chim National Park, home to the sarus crane, the world's largest flying bird, afford travelers a rare glimpse of local wildlife in its natural habitat.

History

From the earliest days of the Dong Son to a thousand-year occupation by the Chinese, centuries of dynastic rule, French colonialism, the rise of Communist revolutionaries, and a tragic war that captured the attention of the world, Vietnam's history has been one of struggle and resilience. The 20th century alone included wars against France, the United States, Cambodia, and China. As a result, nationalism runs deep in Vietnam. Regardless of age, gender, religion, or political opinion, Vietnamese take great pride in their cultural identity and in their perseverance against foreign invaders.

After years of post-war poverty followed by an incredible economic boom, Vietnam has transformed from a small, war-stricken nation into one of Southeast Asia's most promising economies in little more than a few decades. As the country continues to prosper, the government struggles to reconcile its values with the rampant capitalism of Vietnam's urban centers, as well as the environmental impact of its fast-paced development.

ANCIENT CIVILIZATION

While most Western accounts of Vietnamese history tend to focus on more recent events, the earliest inhabitants of the S-shaped country arrived several thousand years ago. In the Mekong Delta, an ancient civilization known as Funan existed from around AD 100 up until the 6th century. The south-central coast was once occupied by Champa, a matriarchal Hindu civilization now remembered for its famous red-brick architecture. From the 2nd century AD to as late as the mid-1600s, the Cham

temple carvings from the ancient Champa era

held an ever-decreasing foothold in the region, farming rice, making pottery, trading with other civilizations, and often engaging in armed conflicts with their neighbors, a fact that led to their eventual demise at the hands of the Vietnamese.

Today's Vietnamese originated in the Red River Delta where, as far back as the first millennium BC, a highly evolved culture known as the Dong Son ran a thriving trade port, developed a complex irrigation system for rice farming, and is now remembered for its intricately patterned bronze drums. Hung Vuong, the first ruler of the Vietnamese people, is believed to have been a Dong Son ruler, though it is difficult to discern exactly when he lived, as the true origins of the Vietnamese people are intertwined with mythology. This dynasty reigned over northern Vietnam and parts of southern China for 18 generations before the throne was usurped by An Duong Vuong in the 3rd century BC.

ONE THOUSAND YEARS UNDER THE CHINESE

In 208 BC, the Chinese invaded northern Vietnam, marking the start of a thousand-year occupation that would deeply influence Vietnamese traditions and culture. At first, the Han dynasty was lax, allowing its colony to function in much the way it always had. But, once the Chinese began to impose high taxes and force the Vietnamese to adopt their traditions and style of dress, resentment flourished among the general population. Across the northern reaches of the country, rebellions were routinely suppressed. The most famous of these, an AD 39 insurrection led by the Trung sisters, drove the Chinese out of Vietnam for just over two years before the northern power returned to reclaim its colony. Following this semi-successful revolt, the Han dynasty gave up all pleasantries, removing Vietnamese lords from power and permitting local aristocrats to occupy only the lowest rungs of the political ladder.

Eventually, after centuries of rule, things began to come undone in China. Growing unrest along the border made it difficult for the northern empire to keep its colony in check. In the far north, minority hill tribes rebelled against Chinese rule, while several Vietnamese aristocrats began claiming a right to the throne. Ultimately, the Tang dynasty fell in China in 907, creating a weakened empire, and Vietnamese general Ngo Quyen swooped in to take independence for his country.

AN INDEPENDENT VIETNAM

Despite Ngo Quyen's victory over the Chinese, his own reign was brief. In less than three decades, the emperor was overthrown. A handful of other short-lived rulers took his place, but it wasn't until the Ly dynasty that the kingdom was able to grow. In 1075, royal officials in Vietnam wrote examinations for the first time, following in the footsteps of the Chinese empire. By 1089, the practice was required, creating a fixed hierarchy of

The Trung Sisters

Two of Vietnam's most celebrated figures, the Trung sisters were a pair of aristocratic women born in Giao Chi, as the country was then called, in the early AD years. Like many at the time, Trung Trac and Trung Nhi opposed Chinese rule, but it wasn't until the husband of the elder sister, a Vietnamese nobleman named Thi Sach, was put to death by Giao Chi's Chinese ruler that the women took action.

In order to avenge Thi Sach's death, the Trung sisters launched a rebellion that unified anti-colonialists against the Giao Chi administration, driving its Chinese ruler out of Vietnam in AD 39. Trung Trac became the nation's queen, her sister a high-ranking second, and the pair briefly held sovereignty over the kingdom until the Chinese returned in AD 42, armed to the teeth and with enough warriors to defeat their enemy. When it became clear that the fight was over and defeat inevitable for the Vietnamese, the sisters jumped into a river and committed suicide. To this day, their name, Hai Ba Trung, appears on street signs across the country and they are revered as an example of fierce nationalism and powerful Vietnamese women.

public officials. At the same time, the Ly dynasty adopted Buddhism as its royal religion, which in turn encouraged Vietnamese subjects to convert.

Southward expansion also began, with the Dai Viet marching out to conquer the Cham kingdom of Vijaya in 1079. An arranged marriage in 1225 ended the Ly dynasty, transferring power from its last remaining princess to the Tran family, who carried on a similar tradition of success. During this time, Kublai Khan and his Mongol army began to eye northern Vietnam, thrice attempting to take over the empire. One of the Tran dynasty's most famous heroes is Tran Hung Dao, the celebrated general who thwarted the Mongols' final attempt at Bach Dang River by impaling his enemy's ships with wooden spikes during low tide.

Following the defeat of the Mongols, the Tran dynasty entered a steady decline. They managed to get in a few more victories over the Cham before a power shift came in 1400, when General Ho Quy Ly overthrew the king and claimed Dai Viet for himself. General Ho's policies proved unfavorable and local landowners appealed to the Chinese for help. China's Ming dynasty promptly returned and reasserted its authority in 1407. This second occupation lasted roughly two decades, with the Chinese exerting their unrestrained power over the Dai Viet. All local customs and traditions were banned, citizens were required to wear Chinese dress, and a particularly harsh forced labor policy came into effect, all of which had a significant impact on local culture for years to come. In 1428, colonization ended thanks to Le Loi, a scholar who had rejected the Ming dynasty's rule and amassed an army to defeat the Chinese. In an attempt to remain civil, he provided the losers with ships and supplies to sail home rather than putting them to death.

Throughout the 15th century, Vietnam's Le dynasty continued to move south, conquering any kingdom that stood in their way. However, as Vietnam's territory expanded, its rulers struggled to maintain control over the newer settlements, which were far-removed from the capital. When a high-ranking official usurped the throne in 1527, two aristocratic families, the Trinh and Nguyen lords, backed the Le dynasty in hopes of sharing their power once the kingdom had been retaken. After 1545, Vietnam found itself divided: the Nguyens controlled the southern half of the country, while the Trinhs took charge of the north.

During this time, European missionaries began to appear in Vietnam, hoping to convert the local population. One of the most famous was French priest Alexandre de Rhodes, who arrived in Indochina in 1619, picked up the local language, and promptly began espousing the benefits of Catholicism to the Vietnamese. By the time he was kicked out of the country in 1630, de Rhodes had converted over 6,000 Vietnamese. He is also credited with the development of the Romanized *quoc ngu* script used by the Vietnamese today.

Down south, the Nguyens ran an agricultural society, keeping uneducated peasants at bay, while the northern Trinh emphasized education and intellectual development. Neither gained a strong following among the masses, as ongoing war, natural disasters, and taxes left the general population frustrated and disillusioned. Rebellions were common, though they were often small and concentrated to a single area, making it easy for both ruling families to silence their opponents. That is until a trio of brothers from Tay Son appeared on the scene.

TAY SON REBELLION

Nguyen Hue, Nguyen Nhac, and Nguyen Lu were three brothers from central Binh Dinh province whose ancestry actually traced back to the short-lived reign of General Ho Quy Ly in 1400. Like many subjects at the time, the brothers were thoroughly displeased with the Nguyen Lords and unimpressed by imperial bureaucracy in general. Initially siding with the Trinhs of the north, the brothers launched a revolt in 1771, intending to overthrow the Nguyen Lords on their own. By the following year, they had successfully taken Binh Dinh and Quang Nam provinces and, with growing support, managed to extend the takeover to all of southern Vietnam by 1778. Operating on a Robin Hood-style mantra, the brothers nixed taxes, set prisoners free, and gave out food to the peasant population. Their progressive policies later moved north, turning on the Trinh Lords and once again fending off the Chinese to rule the entire country, with each brother presiding over a region of Vietnam.

In defeating the southern rulers, the Tay Son rebellion had failed to kill all heirs to the throne: Prince Nguyen Anh, the only remaining Nguyen Lord, fled to Gia Dinh, now known as Ho Chi Minh City, and sought the assistance of Pigneau de Behaine, a French bishop. Shortly thereafter, Pigneau de Behaine sailed to Pondicherry in French India and, later, back to Europe to request the aid of the French king in restoring Nguyen Anh to the throne. Louis XVI agreed, so long as Vietnam would offer up the port of Danang and the Con Dao islands, then known as Poulo Condore, in exchange. But, upon Pigneau de Behaine's return to Pondicherry, the French delegates refused to help. The bishop raised his own funds to hire ships and soldiers, returning to Vietnam in 1789 with enough ammunition to wipe out the Tay Son rebels by 1801, creating a unified Vietnam for the first time in 200 years.

Under newly crowned emperor Gia Long, the country returned to a more conservative imperial rule, with the king undoing many policies enacted by the Nguyen brothers in order to assert his authority. Opposition was strictly punished and many of the previously erased taxes returned. Though there was occasional dissent, it wasn't until the death of emperor Gia Long that France's intention to invade solidified. Gia Long's son Minh Mang, an austere ruler and staunch believer in Confucianism, expelled all European missionaries from Vietnam and set about killing Vietnamese Catholics and any missionaries caught preaching the Bible.

FRENCH COLONIALISM

Convinced that invasion was the best course of action, the French stormed the shores of Danang in 1858, advancing south to take Gia Dinh the following year. Armed with a religious cause—to protect its missionaries—the French had hoped that Vietnamese Catholics would rush to their aid, but no one appeared. Instead, it became clear that the motives for this invasion had nothing to do with Catholicism and everything to do with business and military might. Over the next decade or so, the French managed to acquire all of Vietnam's territory, wresting power from then-emperor Tu Duc by 1874, though the country's colonization wasn't official until 1883.

The Vietnamese were caught between two evils: the French were unpopular for having taken the country by force, but the poor government of emperor Tu Duc and his failure to protect the people from harm had lost him a great deal of public support. In the beginning, some were open to the idea of a new governmental system. But, as it became clear that economic exploitation was part of the plan, the French fell out of favor. Under colonial rule, most Vietnamese were overtaxed, overworked, and abused. While rice exports soared in the colonists' new open economy, all profits went to the European power. Many high-ranking Vietnamese scholars and officials refused to play a part in the colonial government for this reason.

By the turn of the 20th century, dissent sparked rebellions across the country. As World War I raged in Europe, Vietnamese troops were sent abroad in the name of France. Shortly thereafter, Ho Chi Minh arrived in Guangzhou, China, where he founded the Revolutionary Youth League in 1925, attempting to wrangle all of Vietnam's disparate Communist and anti-French parties together. A 1930 conference solidified the main aims of

As a response, the French
bombed the area and sent many of its citizens to jail.

WORLD WAR II

Toward the end of the 1930s, trouble was brewing in Europe on the eve of
World War II, and dissent in its Southeast Asian colonies had France on
edge. In 1941, Ho Chi Minh returned to Vietnam after 30 years abroad
and was welcomed with open arms. When France fell to the Nazis in 1940
and Japanese troops arrived in Vietnam, demanding safe passage of their
military and weapons through the country, Ho Chi Minh's now-famous
resistance army, the Viet Minh, took note of the colonial government's
weakness.

By March 1945, Uncle Ho felt confident enough that he offered the
French an ultimatum: relinquish power or face the consequences. Japan
didn't wait for a response and wrested the country from European hands
that same month, claiming it a free state under Japanese occupation. But
while their Asian neighbors had removed authority from the Europeans,
Vietnam recognized Japan's increasingly dire circumstances on the world
stage and prepared to swoop into the anticipated power vacuum that would
occur when they left. Sure enough, when Japan retreated from Vietnam in
1945, the Viet Minh launched its now-famous August Revolution across the
country, stepping into power for the first time, just as Bao Dai, Vietnam's
last emperor, relinquished his crown. Ho Chi Minh declared independence
on September 2, 1945, in Hanoi.

FRANCO-VIETNAM WAR

The French refused to go quietly. Though Ho Chi Minh's declaration was
met with an overwhelmingly positive response, the Europeans returned to
Vietnam after World War II in hopes of regaining their colonial foothold.
By 1946, it was clear that there would not be a peaceful resolution and both
sides prepared for war. Over nine years, the French and the Viet Minh
duked it out across the country, the former well-armed, the latter boasting heavy manpower. Though France had many Vietnamese cities within
its grasp, the countryside belonged to the Viet Minh, who set up training camps and recruitment centers within its territory. After the People's
Republic of China was officially established in 1949, the Viet Minh were
able to source weapons from the north, a move which gave them the upper
hand. As Vietnamese forces took back northern Vietnam, opening up supply lines and enabling them to attack the Red River Delta, the French began
to lose heart.

Still, by the end of 1953, colonial forces took Dien Bien Phu, a far-off
town in the mountainous northwest, hoping to turn the tide of war by in-
terfering with their enemy's access to supplies. Instead, this was the move
that sealed their fate. In March 1954, two months before diplomatic talks
were set to begin in Geneva, the Viet Minh laid siege to Dien Bien Phu,

bringing in ample artillery and over 100,000 troops to cut off all access to the outside world. By the time the Geneva talks began on May 8, France had surrendered and Ho Chi Minh's army was victorious.

In the resulting accords, which were signed by both Vietnam's Communist government and France, the country was divided in half at the 17th parallel with the promise of reuniting both sides in a 1956 election. While this agreement brought temporary peace and the exodus of Vietnam's colonizers, few—if any—of the parties present during the Geneva talks actually believed that Vietnam would be reunited so seamlessly.

With northern Vietnam now staunchly Communist and the southern Republic of Vietnam in limbo, the United States began to take a vested interest in the country's political situation. Hoping to keep the Communists out of power, they backed Ngo Dinh Diem, a Vietnamese Catholic with little political experience. Over the next two years, Diem exercised strict control over religious groups in the Mekong Delta and quashed any dissent in Saigon. By 1955, Diem openly rejected the elections meant to reunify Vietnam and instead held his own rigged referendum, winning the presidency by a landslide.

Using his own family and connections, Diem fashioned himself a cabinet of leaders and began to rule, making little effort to win over public support. As the 1950s drew to a close, the southern government had become so careless with its power that many of the Communists who had opted to go north after the Geneva Accords returned in order to stage attacks against Diem's government. In the city, regular protests took place. Diem attempted to resettle all south Vietnamese into what he termed "strategic hamlets," an effort to separate average civilians from the NLF rebels fighting against him. These villages turned out to be a breeding ground for NLF converts, as south Vietnamese did not take kindly to leaving their homes and rebel fighters were able to tunnel beneath the hamlets, establishing access to this increasingly disgruntled population.

VIETNAM WAR

By 1963, tensions in south Vietnam had reached a fever pitch: across Saigon, civilians routinely demonstrated against Diem's corrupt government. For his part, the president showed no interest in appeasing his public and carried on in the same disconnected fashion. When the Venerable Thich Quang Duc, senior monk of a Saigonese pagoda, lit himself on fire in the middle of a downtown intersection one morning in June, photos of the scene were splashed across front pages worldwide. In the face of an international outcry, Diem and his cronies remained flippant. Madame Nhu, the wife of Diem's brother and a powerful behind-the-scenes player, famously referred to the event as a "barbecue." However, the military arm of Diem's government saw the writing on the wall and discreetly approached the U.S. government in order to gauge their receptiveness to a coup. They were hardly met with resistance.

By November, the generals of south Vietnam realized their plan, assassinating Diem and his brother, Nhu. The Americans remained neutral on the subject and, less than a month later, President John F. Kennedy met the same fate, shaking up the stability of the American-backed south once more. Newly installed President Johnson took a different approach to his predecessor, sending increased military aid to Vietnam. In 1964, north Vietnamese forces exchanged fire with an American naval ship, prompting the Gulf of Tonkin Resolution, which granted President Johnson the power to take "necessary measures" against the Vietnamese Communists. Air strikes were ordered against the north, but American planes alone could not keep the enemy from advancing. Eventually, ground troops began to pour into Vietnam, their numbers swelling to 485,000 by the end of 1967. Defoliants like Agent Orange were used to destroy the dense jungles where NLF and north Vietnamese forces hid, and heavy bombing ravaged the countryside. Americans at home, meanwhile, began to express their growing disapproval of the war, questioning the role of U.S. troops in the conflict and the increasing civilian casualties.

The 1968 Tet Offensive proved a turning point for the war. On January 31, the eve of the country's biggest holiday, north Vietnamese and NLF forces launched a coordinated attack. Five major cities, 36 provincial capitals, 64 district capitals, and over two dozen airfields were targeted and some taken over by Communist forces. Though U.S. soldiers ultimately regained the territory lost during these attacks, the event did major damage to public sentiment at home, where Americans were being told that victory was imminent. Instead, footage of the Tet battles broadcast on news channels around the world showed a far more dire situation.

In 1969, with troop numbers already exceeding 500,000, President Nixon began to withdraw American soldiers from Vietnam, a move that was met with approval at home but only worsened the low morale of troops left behind. The new president pushed for "Vietnamization," handing over control to south Vietnamese forces. Peace talks were arranged in Paris. But, by 1971, little progress had been made. Meanwhile, news of the My Lai massacre, in which U.S. troops killed hundreds of unarmed Vietnamese in Quang Ngai province, was made public, as were Nixon's secret bombings of Communist bases in Cambodia, both of which fueled public outrage in the United States. Over the next two years, the United States and north Vietnam's Communist government went back and forth at the negotiating table, using military attacks to encourage their adversaries to bargain. On January 27, 1973, the Agreement on Ending the War and Restoring Peace in Vietnam was signed by north Vietnam, south Vietnam, and the United States and a cease-fire went into effect the following day.

By the end of March, the last American military units left Vietnam. Over the next two years, the country continued to suffer casualties as an ineffective south Vietnamese government aimed to win over civilians while its military, with a soaring number of deserters and the NLF hot on their heels, rapidly came undone. The following year, north Vietnamese forces made a push to reclaim the areas they had lost. On April 30, 1975, north Vietnamese tanks crashed through the gates of Saigon's Independence Palace, marking the end of the 30-year conflict.

AFTER 1975

At peace for the first time in 30 years, Vietnam's Communist government found itself faced with a new challenge: how to take a ravaged, war-stricken nation and bring it out of poverty. Still reeling from the after-effects of war and deeply paranoid about the possibility of any more foreign invaders, the country closed itself off from the world. This proved to be a justifiable concern, as brief border skirmishes with China and a two-year war with Cambodia followed; both conflicts were resolved by the end of 1979. Meanwhile, South Vietnam supporters were sent to study sessions and re-education camps, essentially hard labor outfits, in order to restructure southern society to match the wishes of the northern government. Surveillance was heavy throughout the country, as the new government worked hard to squash any and all dissent. A central economy, built on austerity, steered people forward over the next decade or so, but it soon became clear that this government-run system was doing nothing to bring the average Vietnamese out of abject poverty.

For this reason, the government instituted *doi moi* in the mid-1980s, a series of economic reforms which eventually transitioned Vietnam to a market economy. As 1990 approached, the country began to open itself up again to the world. These reforms became the saving grace of Vietnam: in just two decades, *doi moi* took Vietnam's poverty rate from 60 percent of the population to 17 percent.

Government and Economy

GOVERNMENT

The Socialist Republic of Vietnam is a one-party Communist state. Its legislative body, the National Assembly, consists of 500 representatives who meet twice a year and are elected for five-year terms by popular vote. This organization has the power to both make and amend the country's laws, as well as its constitution, and is responsible for voting in the government's highest officials, including the president and prime minister. Both of these offices belong to the Politburo (executive branch) and are among the highest positions of power in the country. In addition to the president, the highest office in Vietnam, and the prime minister he appoints, several other ministers are proposed by the prime minister for specific areas such as finance, education and training, foreign affairs and public security, and later approved by the National Assembly, rounding out the rest of the high-ranking cabinet. Both the president and the prime minister can serve up to two terms.

Elections

Elections for National Assembly delegates are held once every five years. This is the only governmental body to be selected by popular vote, but due to the fact that Vietnam is a one-party state, there is little difference from one candidate to another. Still, these elected officials—Party members who have been chosen for the public to select—are responsible for voting in a president, who later has the power to select a prime minister.

ECONOMY

While Vietnam's economy took a rocky turn after the American War, stifled by strict centralized policies, the *doi moi* economic reforms of the mid-1980s opened the country up to international trade and industrial development. Once a solely agricultural society, industry has made its way into the country, with plenty of foreign enterprises setting up offices in major cities, particularly Ho Chi Minh City. Vietnam has become an especially attractive destination for foreign firms to outsource work in garment and textile production, as well as electronics and food processing. Though growth has slowed somewhat in recent years the country continues to make economic gains, albeit at a slower rate.

Today, much of Vietnam's wealth is concentrated in urban areas along the coast. The majority of Vietnam's rapidly growing middle class lives here, where greater work and educational opportunities are available. Rural areas remain at a disadvantage. Family members who move away from the countryside or overseas often remit part of their salary back to these rural communities as financial assistance—Vietnam is one of the top-10 remittance-receiving nations in the world. As economic growth slows in Vietnam, its poorest citizens remain in very remote areas where infrastructure is weak and access to education, job opportunities, and even basic necessities is limited. In the mountainous northern and interior regions, this lack of infrastructure and opportunity tends to affect minority communities more heavily than their ethnic Vietnamese counterparts. Meanwhile, a select group of urban Vietnamese are considered ultra-wealthy, boasting a net worth of USD$30 million or more, highlighting the country's growing income disparity.

People and Culture

DEMOGRAPHY

Though Vietnam is composed of 54 separate ethnic groups, the Kinh (ethnic Vietnamese) make up an overwhelming 87 percent of the population, which is now an estimated 91.7 million. Thanks to this rapid growth, a two-child rule is loosely in effect throughout Vietnam; while it is seldom enforced, you'll see signs across the country encouraging families to stop at two babies. Vietnam is an incredibly literate society, with over 90 percent of the country able to read and write.

The majority of Vietnam's population lives on or near the coast, leaving the more remote mountain areas for the country's ethnic minorities, once known to the French as *montagnards,* an array of small, tight-knit groups that still lead traditional farming lives and practice many of the same customs as their ancestors. In the Mekong Delta, a healthy Khmer community lives among the region's Kinh farmers, practicing their own brand of Buddhism, as do small, isolated groups of Islamic Cham. The mountainous areas of the Central Highlands are inhabited by the Gia Rai, E De, and Churu, among other groups, while the soaring peaks around Sapa and the rest of the northwest are home to the Dao, Giay, Thai, and H'mong people, each with their own language, culture, and traditions. While these are some of the most diverse areas in the country, they are also the least developed and, in many cases, the poorest.

RELIGION

Vietnam is a largely Mahayana Buddhist country, with most people paying a visit to the local pagoda every few weeks. The country's religious beliefs are deeply influenced by Chinese beliefs, with traces of Taoism and Confucianism. Thanks to its former European ties, a strong Catholic following also exists, though their numbers are nowhere near as great as the Buddhist community. Several smaller, homegrown religions were invented in the 20th century in the Mekong Delta area, including Caodaism, a syncretic faith in which Victor Hugo and Elvis are considered saints, and Hoa Hao, which amassed a large following in the mid-1900s but later faded out after its military involvement in the Franco-Vietnam War.

Vietnamese culture includes a strong spiritual aspect, and most locals believe in worshipping their ancestors. In addition to the many pagodas and Catholic churches throughout the country, the vibrant Caodaist temples, and even a small collection of local mosques, Vietnam boasts several temples in honor of national heroes and those considered collective ancestors of the Vietnamese people.

LANGUAGE

Vietnamese is the nation's official language and features a mind-boggling six tones and 11 vowel sounds. Though it was originally written in

Death Rituals

Vietnam's approach to death is different than that of the Western world. Regardless of religion, Vietnamese believe in ancestor worship. These include blood relatives as well as collective national ancestors like Ho Chi Minh or Tran Hung Dao. When a Vietnamese person passes away, it is believed that one's life does not end but that the afterlife begins. The afterlife requires basic necessities, such as food, clothing, and money, all of which a family must provide for its deceased loved ones. In most homes, shops, and businesses, you'll find a small altar where local residents put food, beverages, and occasionally cigarettes for the dead. These offerings are often accompanied by prayers and incense. On holidays and certain Buddhist festivals, Vietnamese burn paper money and clothing for their ancestors to use in the afterlife. While it's bad luck for the living to keep these items, you'll likely spot stray hundred dollar bills on the sidewalk or in the streets. Though they're flimsier than the actual currency, these paper notes are surprisingly accurate—until you turn them over to find the phrase "Bank of the Dead" instead of "In God We Trust."

Beyond these ongoing rituals, Vietnamese funerals are a multi-day affair meant to usher a loved one into the afterlife. When a Vietnamese person dies, his or her family will mourn for several days, inviting friends and family as well as a religious leader to say goodbye. Mourners often wear white headbands. The funeral, held at home, usually includes a large tent set up in front of the building for guests to visit. An altar, complete with offerings and portrait of the deceased, is set up inside. At the end of the mourning period, the body is placed in a coffin and carried to its final resting place in a large, truck-like hearse, usually decorated with colorful symbols; some Vietnamese are cremated. This final procession begins before sunrise, sometimes as early as 4am or 5am, and often involves music. Don't be surprised if you wake up in the wee hours of the morning to trumpets and crashing cymbals—this is simply someone on their way to the afterlife.

Once the funeral is complete, Vietnamese carry on providing the essentials for their ancestors through offerings. The day of a person's death, rather than his or her birth, is remembered and celebrated as a holiday. This occasion, called *dam gio,* is a family event, in which members of that particular house come together and give offerings to their deceased relative, visit with family and friends, and often make trips to the local pagoda or church to commemorate the individual. Contrary to Western ideas of death, *dam gio* is not a somber occasion but rather a celebration of that individual and his or her life.

a modified version of Chinese characters, known as *chu nom,* European missionary Alexandre de Rhodes developed a Roman script for the language that is now used throughout the country, making Vietnam one of the only nations in mainland Southeast Asia to use a Roman alphabet. Throughout Vietnam, three major regional dialects are spoken, with the northern Hanoian dialect considered the most authentic Vietnamese thanks to its short, succinct tonal pronunciation. The southern and central regions of the country also have their own respective dialects: You'll find a slower, more fluid accent in Ho Chi Minh City and the Mekong Delta,

Vietnam is one of the only nations in Southeast Asia to use the Roman alphabet.

while central Vietnam is known for its creative pronunciation and a slew of unique regional vocabulary. Among Vietnamese, the central accent is considered the most difficult to understand, with many native speakers straining to converse with those from cities like Hue or Hoi An.

Beyond Vietnamese, an array of languages are spoken among the country's ethnic minorities in their respective homelands. These languages are rarely heard on the coast, and all public transactions are conducted in Vietnamese. Ethnic minority citizens must learn Vietnamese as a second language in order to participate fully in society.

The Arts

VISUAL ARTS

Vietnamese visual art draws upon an interesting variety of mediums and influences, thanks to its past relationships with China and France. Particularly over the last century, traditional handicrafts like lacquer painting and enamel have been combined with both Asian and European ideas to create uniquely Vietnamese artwork. While many of the masterpieces displayed in forums like the local fine arts museum are prime examples of traditional Vietnamese artwork, both Hanoi and Saigon have small but deep-rooted contemporary art scenes and plenty of up-and-coming artists whose work is shared in local cafés and smaller galleries.

MUSIC

Traditional Vietnamese music is often closely linked with theatrical performance: *cheo,* a centuries-old satirical form of theater, uses music to communicate its messages, as does *cai luong,* a similarly operatic form of music from the south that had its heyday during the 20th century. For most locals today, famous revolutionary composers such as Trinh Cong Son, one of Vietnam's most prolific songwriters, and Pham Duy remain favorites among many Vietnamese, both old and young. Their songs are regular fixtures during karaoke sessions.

Beyond traditional music, the younger generation is following its Asian neighbors, eager to develop a V-Pop phenomenon similar to Japan or Korea, with plenty of doe-eyed young songstresses and flashy music videos making the rounds on the Internet. Music-related television shows like *Vietnam Idol* and *The Voice of Vietnam,* knock-offs of their American counterparts, are also popular, as is the famed program *Paris By Night,* a much-loved musical revue filmed in France, Canada, and the United States.

Essentials

Getting There

FROM NORTH AMERICA

Travelers may enter Vietnam by air through its three largest airports: **Tan Son Nhat International Airport** (SGN) in Ho Chi Minh City; **Noi Bai International Airport** (HAN) in Hanoi; and **Danang International Airport** (DAD) in Danang. From there, plenty of smaller regional airports serve the more remote areas of Vietnam.

The most expensive part of your trip to Vietnam will be the plane ticket. Even bargain fares across the Pacific are not cheap. Still, there are a couple of strategies to make your airfare as affordable as possible. Websites like **Kayak** (www.kayak.com), **Sky Scanner** (www.skyscanner.com), and **Expedia** (www.expedia.com) offer travelers a comprehensive range of airlines. When booking through these sites, monitor airfare prices 6-8 weeks in advance. While prices may fluctuate to some degree, USD$100-200 either way, round-trip tickets hover at about USD$1,000. Those leaving from the West Coast of the United States will find slightly cheaper fares; East Coasters and anyone traveling from the middle of the continental United States should expect four-figure prices.

It is sometimes possible to save money by flying into Los Angeles International Airport (LAX) with a budget airline and then heading for Asia from there. When traveling to Vietnam, most routes pass over the Pacific, connecting to Ho Chi Minh City or Hanoi in major hubs like Seoul, Hong Kong, Tokyo, or Taipei. A few airlines go the opposite direction, passing through Europe and the Middle East.

While dirt-cheap fares are offered by carriers like China Eastern and China Southern, these companies are not known for their service or safety ratings. Carriers like EVA, Japan Air, Emirates, Cathay Pacific, United, Singapore Airlines, and Qatar Airlines all serve Vietnam's major airports and, for a few extra dollars, are reliable, professional, and usually more comfortable (particularly important for a 14-hour flight).

FROM NEIGHBORING COUNTRIES

Vietnam shares several foreigner-friendly overland border crossings with its neighbors: five with Cambodia, six with Laos, and three with China. These crossings are fairly straightforward but, like any point of entry into Vietnam, you are required to obtain a valid visa prior to arrival. With the exception of e-visa processing, which is only available at the country's three largest airports, no crossing in Vietnam will supply you with a visa at the border gate. Regularly scheduled buses pass through the country's frontier areas on a daily basis and often provide service to major cities

Previous: Hanoi street food; freeway sign.

in neighboring countries. There are no international railways linking Vietnam to its neighbors.

Several budget airlines fly to and from Vietnam. Direct flights depart from major regional airports in Bangkok, Kuala Lumpur, Hong Kong, and Singapore, as well as Yangon and Taipei. For other destinations, connecting flights go through the aforementioned hubs from dozens of destinations within Southeast Asia. Airfare from neighboring countries is usually reasonable.

DISCOUNT TICKETS

Regional budget airlines such as **VietJet** (www.vietjetair.com), **Air Asia** (www.airasia.com), **Jetstar** (www.jetstar.com), and **Tiger Air** (www.tigerair.com) serve Southeast Asia's major airports, including those in Thailand, Cambodia, China, Laos, Malaysia, Myanmar, and Vietnam. VietJet, the country's only homegrown budget airline, covers even the most remote destinations in Vietnam as well as an ever-expanding network of international destinations throughout Asia. Air Asia's network is also extensive, providing connecting flights from across the region, while Tiger Air and Jetstar both fly to Australia and a handful of Southeast Asian nations. These are the most affordable of the bunch, but most budget airlines within the region tack on additional fees for just about everything; read the fine print when booking these fares.

ORGANIZED TOURS

In any given tourist destination, there are dozens of companies offering organized day trips and multi-day tours. The majority of Vietnam's cheaper travel outfits follow the same tourist trail, offering cookie-cutter itineraries that present little in the way of authenticity or spontaneity. Larger companies have day trips for as little as VND100,000; these trips provide an easy way to meet other travelers, but the tours themselves are not groundbreaking. In most cases, if you're up for the challenge it's more worthwhile to make the trip on your own. For certain excursions (treks in Sapa, for example), hiring a guide and paying the extra cash is recommended to make the most of your time.

More independent tour outfits are popping up all the time. Many of these private companies have done great things for the country's tourism image, providing foreign travelers with exciting, worthwhile experiences that also benefit the local community. While prices are higher, these customized tour outfits are usually affordable when split between several people and the level of service is a cut above what you would find in a larger, corporate tour company.

AIR

Within Vietnam, there are three main airlines with domestic routes: the national carrier **Vietnam Airlines** (www.vietnamairlines.com); as well as two budget ventures, Australian company **Jetstar** (www.jetstar.com) and local outfit **VietJet** (www.vietjetair.com). For cheap fares, VietJet is a touch more reliable than Jetstar. Vietnam Airlines, though more expensive, serves the widest range of destinations, including some of the more remote airports in Vietnam. The national carrier also has exclusive access to certain areas, such as the remote Con Dao Islands.

RAIL

Vietnam's main railway runs from Saigon to Hanoi along the coast, with major stops in Nha Trang and Danang. While some of these trains have seen better days, the sleeper cars are reasonably comfortable, though more expensive than sleeper buses, which, while slightly less safe, run more frequently. Trains are a great way to complete any long-distance journey, particularly with so many overnight routes offered, as you can spend a bit more money on train fare in exchange for saving on a hotel bill. There are a handful of destinations to which a train ride is even preferable over other options, particularly in the mountainous north, where winding roads make for a less-than-pleasant bus ride. The website **Man in Seat 61** (www.seat61.com) is an indispensable source of information on train travel within Vietnam and Southeast Asia.

BUS

The cheapest way to get around in-country is by bus. Vietnam has an extensive system of roadways and dozens of tourist bus companies featuring both seated and sleeper vehicles, which run regularly along the length of the coast, from Hanoi and its surrounding areas all the way south to the Mekong Delta and into neighboring countries. Many tourists get around on buses, though certain routes—from Hue to Hanoi, for instance, or the drive up to Sapa—are more dangerous than others. In these cases, it's better to travel via train, motorbike, or hired vehicle.

In most major cities there is a bus station serving both nearby and long-distance destinations. Safe and reliable tickets are available through many of the more well-known travel companies, like **Sinh Tourist** (www.thesinhtourist.com) and **Phuong Trang** (www.futabuslines.com.vn). When booking tickets, deal with the larger, more reputable bus lines rather than smaller, cheaper companies, as the few dollars you may save on a local bus could wind up costing you time as a result of breakdowns or other troubles.

While buses are an affordable and convenient way to travel within Vietnam, theft sometimes occurs, particularly on overnight buses. Take care when traveling to keep your belongings with you at all times, either in your lap or very close to your person. Sadly, more than a few travelers have taken an overnight bus only to wake up at their destination with one or more of their possessions missing.

TAXI

Even many of Vietnam's smaller cities are equipped with taxi services, and cabs are usually so abundant that it isn't necessary to call an operator or arrange a pick-up unless you're in a remote area. Travelers should have no problem flagging down taxis in the street. The most reputable nationwide company is **Mailinh**, though there are dozens of smaller independent companies in various cities. While some of these cabs are more reliable than others, always check for a proper meter. Base rates for taxis in most major cities run VND10,000-15,000, with fares increasing incrementally based on the distance traveled. Never bargain with a driver for your fare, as this is not to your advantage.

RIDE-HAILING APPS

In recent years, transportation apps have come on the scene in urban Vietnam, upending the local taxi industry, not to mention the widespread use of traditional *xe om*. These services are mainly available in Hanoi and Saigon, where you'll find both **Uber** (www.uber.com) and Malaysian transportation app **Grab** (www.grab.com) in operation. These services are safe and reliable, though few drivers speak English. Still, it's worth booking a Grab or an Uber if you're trying to keep costs down: A motorbike ride on either of these services can go for as little as VND10,000. On both apps, you can hail either a private car or a motorbike.

XE OM

Xe om (motorbike taxis) are a popular and inexpensive means of transportation used throughout the country. Drivers—usually men—perch atop their vehicles on street corners near public parks or in busy tourist areas, waiting to ferry passengers to their preferred destinations around town. As a foreigner, you'll no doubt come into contact with at least a few of these two-wheeled vehicles and their drivers, as *xe om* drivers often call out to passing pedestrians in order to drum up business. Don't be surprised if you hear a "YOU! Motorbiiiiike!" or *"Xe om! Xe om!"* as you approach a street corner, even if you're not looking for a ride.

While *xe om* are an easy and affordable way to get around, most foreign visitors also find them to be a hair-raising experience. *Xe om* drivers, like Manhattan cabbies, move at their own pace, which is usually breakneck, and defy most of the laws of physics, not to mention traffic. *Xe om* are a good way to experience the true pulse of major cities like Saigon or Hanoi and a much faster alternative to cars, thanks to their ability to weave deftly through traffic. While the "helmets" provided by *xe om* drivers would probably prove useless in an accident, it's required by law to wear one. Even if you are advised otherwise, it's important to insist upon some headgear, at least when in the city. Voice your concern if you feel unsafe aboard a *xe om*.

When taking a *xe om*, have the address of your destination written down, as not every driver speaks English, and always agree upon a price before you set off. *Xe om* fares are open to negotiation. Feel free to haggle, but once you've settled on the price stand firm. Drivers will sometimes continue to negotiate their fee once you've already hopped on. If you stand your ground and stick to the original agreement then your *xe om* driver will usually lay off.

With few qualifications required beyond a motorbike license and a full tank of gas, *xe om* drivers are a mixed bag: There are many honest, hard-working men who make a living this way, but, like any profession, there are also a few bad apples. For this reason, it is strongly recommended that you opt for taxis over *xe om* when traveling at night, as it's not unheard of for passengers to be robbed or even thrown off a motorbike after dark, and the *xe om* driver is sometimes in on the deal. Be careful when heading back to your hotel after a night on the town, as it's also possible that your *xe om* driver has had as much to drink as you have. Never hop on a motorbike with someone who appears to be intoxicated—the streets of Vietnam can be dangerous enough as it is.

MOTORBIKE RENTALS

Affordable motorbike rentals are available in major tourist destinations throughout Vietnam. Rates usually hover around VND80,000-200,000 per day, depending on the vehicle. All motorbike rentals should come with a helmet. Stick to recommended rental companies or ask around to find a reliable business. Rental companies often require some type of collateral—a down payment or, in some cases, a passport—before loaning out a bike in order to guarantee that their vehicle will be returned in good condition. This is usually not a problem, but beware that businesses have been known to tack on additional fees after they have your passport in their possession. To save yourself a headache, stick to recommended businesses only, check the brakes and gas gauge of your vehicle before you go, and, like any transaction in Vietnam, make sure that both you and the rental company are clear on the terms of your agreement before setting off.

In most cases, daily rentals are intended for use in or around the city. Barring certain exceptions, like the short trip between Hoi An and Danang or the drive from Nha Trang to Dai Lanh beach, you should not take a daily rental outside the city limits. If you plan to travel on the highway, inform the rental company of your intentions, as you may find yourself in hot water should anything happen to the bike while you're on the road.

When traveling long distances, such as the trip from Hanoi to Saigon (or vice versa), it's also possible to purchase a motorbike. Indeed, many travelers come to Vietnam, buy a heavy-duty vehicle, drive the length of the country, and then sell the motorbike once they've reached their destination. Particularly in Saigon and Hanoi, road-ready vehicles are often on sale in the backpacker neighborhoods, and you should have no trouble buying or selling a motorbike in these destinations.

HIRED CARS

Cars and minibuses can be hired in Vietnam and are widely available. These rental vehicles come with a driver, as foreigners are not permitted to operate a vehicle without a local license. The going rate for a hired car varies depending on the vehicle and its provider. Wherever you rent a car or minibus, be clear about the exact terms of the rental agreement, including which fees are included and which are not, before driving off.

DRIVING IN VIETNAM

Vietnamese law requires all motorists to have a local license, essentially making it illegal for tourists to drive. Though enforcement of the law varies, it is illegal to drive in Vietnam without a Vietnamese license. Most expats don't have a license and many Vietnamese people also operate a vehicle without one. Traveling in the countryside, you can see boys as young as 11 or 12 zipping by on a Honda Wave.

People drive while texting, fail to use the correct turn signals (if they use them at all), routinely speed in the opposite direction down a one-way street, and generally disregard lane markings. Vehicles must drive on the right side of the road, with motorbikes staying in the far right lane at all times. Turning right on a red light is illegal—though it's a common practice in Saigon and seldom enforced by police in the southern hub. While the noise is unpleasant, honking is often a means of defensive driving, an announcement of the vehicle's presence. Beyond that, pay extra attention to larger vehicles when driving, as public buses, taxis, and transport trucks will not hesitate to play chicken with a motorbike.

While it is less likely for foreign drivers to be pulled over by law enforcement (except in large cities like Hanoi and HCMC), it does happen. Most traffic police don't usually go to the trouble of fining foreigners, though this has become more common in Saigon as local authorities become more fluent in English. If you are stopped by the police, remain calm and polite. The proper legal course of action for an unlicensed driver is to impound the motorbike and fine the individual, but this almost never happens. Instead, money often changes hands.

VISAS

All foreign visitors to Vietnam are required to obtain a visa prior to arrival, a process that can be completed up to six months in advance of your trip. For non-American passport holders, tourist visas are available in one- and three-month increments and offer both single- and multiple-entry options. Prices for these visas range from US$25 to US$50.

For Americans, the same visa options are available, though with added complexities. In 2016, Vietnam introduced a **one-year visa** for American passport holders at a cost of USD$135-220, which accompanies the preexisting one- and three-month visa options. Depending on the duration of your visa and where you apply for it—whether through your local embassy or consulate, or via an online service—costs run USD$75-180 for visas in one-, three- and six-month increments, while the yearlong visa will set you back as much as USD$220.

If you are entering the country by land, you can arrange a visa through one of Vietnam's many embassies or consulates in neighboring countries (there are several in Laos and Cambodia) in a matter of a few business days. Visa fees tend to vary depending upon the specific office providing the paperwork, so it's best to inquire about costs at your local embassy or consulate.

Things are simpler for non-Americans, who are able to apply for either a 30- or 90-day tourist visa. Thirty-day visas cost around USD$75-80 for a single-entry stamp and roughly USD$120-135 for a multiple-entry stamp. Ninety-day visas run around USD$100-110 for a single entry and USD$145-160 for multiple entries. Check the official costs with your local embassy, as they change frequently. Tourist visas can also be arranged in the United States by applying in person at the Vietnamese embassy or any one of its consulates, or by sending in the necessary documents and fees by mail. Expedited services are available at a premium. All visa fees rendered outside of Vietnam, whether in the United States or abroad, must be paid in U.S. dollars.

Once in Vietnam, tourists may extend a 30-day visa for up to 60 days by visiting any travel agency that provides visa services. Extensions are also available for 90-day visas, but they are more expensive and generally reserved for emergency situations. Though the extension stamp officially costs about USD$10, the going rate at local travel agencies is around USD$40 for the 30-day visa extension and can reach as high as USD$80 for a monthlong extension of the 90-day visa. This is an unavoidable expense, as the extension process requires the assistance of a Vietnamese speaker, and attempting to complete the process on your own is all but impossible.

If you're entering the country by air, you can save time and money by applying for e-visa processing. This is the most cost-effective option for visitors coming to Vietnam directly from the United States. You will not find information on e-visa processing through the country's official government websites. Vietnamese immigration does not openly advertise this service, but at each of the country's three international airports you will find an official e-visa kiosk through which plenty of travelers have safely and legitimately entered Vietnam.

E-visas can be obtained by contacting a travel agent within the country, many of which provide visa-on-arrival services. You will be asked to supply an image of the identification page in your passport, and within 2-4 business days a letter of approval will be sent to your email. This letter should be two pages: one declaring that you are approved for a visa and the other bearing your name, nationality, and passport number. Upon arrival in Vietnam, you will be required to provide this letter along with a passport photo and a stamping fee, which costs USD$25-50 for 30- and 90-day visas and USD$135 for the yearlong visa offered to American passport holders. An immigration official will then supply you with a visa sticker and send you to the customs line. Along with the stamping fee, you will have to pay an additional fee (usually USD$15-30) to the company providing your letter of approval. All of these costs must be covered in U.S. dollars, including the stamping fee at the airport.

While there are dozens of websites providing e-visa services, exercise caution when applying. There are many safe and reliable websites that provide travelers with legitimate letters of approval, but it is still wise to research reputable companies.

EMBASSIES AND CONSULATES

Within the United States, Vietnam has consular services in several cities, particularly near large communities of overseas Vietnamese. In addition to the **Vietnamese embassy** (1233 20th St. NW, Ste. 400, 202/861-0737, www.vietnamembassy-usa.org, 9:30am-noon and 2:30pm-5pm Mon.-Fri.) in Washington DC, there are also consulates in **San Francisco** (1700 California St., Ste. 580, 415/922-1707, www.vietnamconsulate-sf.org, 8:30am-noon and 2pm-4pm Mon.-Fri.), **Houston** (5251 Westheimer Rd., Ste. 1100, 713/850-1233, www.vietnamconsulateinhouston.org, 9am-noon Mon.-Fri., afternoons by appointment only), and **New York City** (866 UN Plaza, Ste. 428, 212/644-0594, www.vnconsul-ny.org, 9am-5:30pm Mon.-Fri.). Each of these offices provides visa services. The hours listed here are only for telephone inquiries; any in-person applications must take place in the morning, 9:30am-noon.

The United States has an **embassy in Hanoi** (170 Ngoc Khanh, 2nd fl.,

D Ba Dinh, tel. 04/2850-5000, www.vietnam.usembassy.gov) and a **consulate in Ho Chi Minh City** (4 Le Duan, D1, tel. 08/3520-4200, www.ho-chiminh.usconsulate.gov), which are able to help American citizens in the event of an emergency. Any visa problems relating to your stay in Vietnam are better dealt with by a travel agent, as American consular services cannot assist citizens in arranging Vietnamese visas. Both the embassy and the consulate have separate hours for specific services; check their websites before paying either office a visit.

BORDER CROSSINGS

Border crossings in Vietnam are fairly straightforward. The only way to enter or exit overland is by bus, as there are no international trains connecting Vietnam to its neighbors. Frequent buses travel through Vietnam's many border gates, at which time you pass through two sets of border control offices: one for Vietnam and one for the country you are entering or exiting.

POLICE

The police in Vietnam do not have a stellar reputation. A 2013 survey by anti-corruption nonprofit Transparency International found that 37 percent of the Vietnamese population considers local law enforcement the most corrupt institution in the country. A large part of this stems from the fact that most police officers are underpaid and use traffic violations and other infractions as a way to line their pockets. Politicians have vowed to crack down on such behavior, even discussing a possible salary increase in order to deter both law enforcement and government officials from taking bribes; however, the practice remains common. Most cops steer clear of foreign visitors, in large part because of the language barrier. If you need to contact the police, have a Vietnamese speaker on hand, as few officers speak English.

BRIBES

It's rare for foreigners to have to deal with bribery during their trip. The only instance in which a traveler may be required to supply a bribe is at a police checkpoint, where traffic violations are meted out. Since it is illegal for anyone to drive in Vietnam without a local driver's license, if you are pulled over by a police officer, you will have to pay a "fine." In these instances, good manners and a little patience can help to minimize the dent in your wallet, but you will undoubtedly have to part with some cash. Refusing to pay the bribe is a bad idea. Legally, the police are allowed to impound your motorbike if you fail to provide a license. It is unlikely that the traffic authorities will actually do so, but don't call their bluff.

ESSENTIALS
VISAS AND OFFICIALDOM

Accommodations

Throughout Vietnam, accommodations run the gamut from dingy budget hostels to luxurious high-end resorts, sometimes even within the same neighborhood. While there are plenty of good beds available at any price, certain rules hold true for most accommodations. Thanks to the size and volume of many of Vietnam's coastal cities, for instance, noise levels should always be considered when booking, as rooms closer to the ground floor tend to be much louder than rooms higher up, and the same goes for street-facing accommodations versus those in the back of the building. Windows are not a given; it's customary for travelers to ask to see a hotel room before committing to stay the night. A few other amenities, such as elevators, are not always included, but hot water and air-conditioning typically come standard with a room.

Furthermore, though public double-occupancy rates are listed in this book, it is often possible to secure a discount from hotels or guesthouses depending on the season, the length of your stay, and the number of rooms available. Many hotels and guesthouses in larger cities use online reservation sites like Agoda or Booking.com, which can sometimes work to the traveler's advantage by providing cheaper rates, though there are a handful of accommodations that cost more when booking online. For the best price, consult both the hotel directly and their online booking site when available.

When you check in to a hotel in Vietnam you will often be asked to hand over your passport. This is often a source of worry among travelers, but holding one's passport is common practice in Vietnam. Since hotels are required by law to register their guests with the police, many will hold your passport at the front desk during your stay, partly for the authorities and partly for insurance that you don't walk out on your bill (these things occasionally happen). It is acceptable to request that your passport is returned to you after the receptionist has filled out your registration form, though you may be asked to pay in advance.

MAKING RESERVATIONS

Depending upon your location and the time of year, the need for booking accommodations may vary. Most major cities in Vietnam do not require a reservation. With such an abundance of hotels and guesthouses in places like Ho Chi Minh City's Pham Ngu Lao area and the Old Quarter of Hanoi, travelers will never find themselves out in the cold. If you prefer to stay in nicer accommodations and would rather not do the door-to-door legwork, then booking a room is recommended. Be sure when making a reservation that you ask the price up front, as rates may change, and take care to confirm your reservation at least once before arriving at the hotel. Even online sites like Agoda and Booking.com, while reliable, can sometimes make mistakes or lose reservations.

You'll find all manner of accommodations that refer to themselves as *khach san* (hotels). These tend to be larger buildings with more rooms. There is a star rating issued by the Vietnamese government each year, but the criteria for the rating seems to focus on the size of the building rather than the quality of the accommodations. Two- to four-star accommodations are a mixed bag, with plenty of outstanding rooms as well as deteriorating facilities. Boutique and privately owned hotels are usually more impressive, though these are often more expensive, too. Depending upon the rates and quality of the hotel, amenities vary from as little as a bed, air-conditioning, and a hot shower to safety deposit boxes, in-room computers, and fresh fruit or complimentary breakfast.

GUESTHOUSES

Almost interchangeable with budget hotels, Vietnam's guesthouses *(nha nghi)* are smaller versions of the same lodgings, often providing 5-6 rooms where a budget hotel might have 10-12. In general, amenities at a guesthouse include air-conditioning, hot water, and sometimes a refrigerator or TV. These places tend to be the most bare-bones and often the most affordable.

HOSTELS

Hostels and dormitory accommodations are only popular in Vietnam's major cities. While there are a handful of these lodgings in Saigon, Hanoi, and a couple other coastal cities, only one or two hostels actually stand out. All dormitory lodgings should come with proper bedding and a secure locker for each guest, and many also include en suite bathrooms, which limits the number of people sharing a shower.

HOMESTAYS

While there are still plenty of authentic homestays throughout Vietnam, particularly in the Mekong Delta, this is an interesting term nowadays, as "homestay" is often conflated with "guesthouse." Bar a few exceptions, most homestay accommodations are akin to a remote guesthouse, offering the added benefit of home-cooked meals and a bit of interaction with locals, though not as much as you might expect. A growing number of high-end "homestays" are cropping up in more heavily touristed areas—Hoi An, for example; these take on the feel of a bed-and-breakfast, offering more of a local connection along with fancier accommodations.

CAMPING

Camping in Vietnam can have a few different meanings. You may find yourself in a one-room beachside bungalow, a log cabin in the woods, or a tent on the ground. While the lodgings vary, most of these accommodations are located either in national parks or on beaches across the country. Pitching a tent just anywhere is not accepted. In more remote areas, travelers may be able to get away with overnighting in their own accommodations, but along the coast you'll be hard-pressed to find a place to set up camp. In designated areas, camping fees tend to be inexpensive.

Food

Some of the freshest, most flavorful, and most varied dishes in Southeast Asia belong to Vietnam. From Hanoi's *bun cha* (grilled pork in fish sauce with noodles) to Hue's *bun bo* (spicy beef noodle soup) or the dozens of southern meals unique to each small village and town, Vietnamese cuisine's complex and irresistible flavors win over many a hungry traveler. Most meals consist of a rice or noodle base, a few fresh greens, and either meat or tofu. Portions tend to be smaller here than in Western countries. With the cost of meals so low, there's usually room for seconds in the budget.

STREET FOOD

You can't make it to the end of any city block in Vietnam without encountering a street food vendor. Meals are everywhere: in the park; on the sidewalk; outside of government buildings and public meeting areas. Men and women push metal carts down the road or hustle along with a bamboo pole slung over one shoulder. At first glance, the setup appears to be nothing special, but take a closer look and you'll be amazed by what someone can do with a portable stove and a pair of chopsticks.

While you can buy anything from hot bowls of soup to quick sandwiches or smaller snacks for the road, there are a handful of dishes more commonly found on the street than in a restaurant. Sticky rice *(xoi)*, for example, is a popular street-side snack; the rice is often cooked in different leaves or with certain ingredients that turn the rice green, purple, orange, or black. This snack can be served sweet with sugar, coconut, and mung bean, or savory, often accompanied by chicken. A handful of other sweets, including a hot tofu dessert with ginger and tapioca or fried rice cakes with mung bean, are also found on street carts or in a basket on someone's head.

There is something to be said for cooking your food out in the open: Street food kitchens, while simple, are almost always more transparent. You're able to tell which vendors are clean and which are not.

REGIONAL FOODS

While dishes like pho, Vietnam's national soup, and *banh mi* (Vietnamese sandwiches) come standard almost everywhere, local fare is divided into three main regions: the north, central, and south. Shaped in large part by its weather and surroundings, each region's cuisine relies upon both rice and fish sauce as main staples but also has its own distinguishing characteristics. Furthermore, nearly every hamlet and every village across the country has its own unique recipes.

Northern fare is more meat-heavy, shying away from seafood in favor

The Stranger Side of Vietnamese Cuisine

In a nation as food-focused as Vietnam, it is all but impossible to come up with dozens of savory masterpieces without having created a few strange dishes along the way. While pho and *banh mi* (Vietnamese sandwiches) have gained worldwide acclaim as delicious, accessible facets of local cuisine, there are several specialties that manage to make some travelers wrinkle their noses.

Century eggs: A traditional Chinese delicacy that has carried over to Vietnam, century eggs are regular chicken or duck eggs that have been preserved in a combination of clay, ash, salt, lime, and rice for several weeks, during which time the pH of the egg elevates, changing the yolk to a dark green, creamy ball at the center of a gelatinous brown egg. The resulting dish is slightly off-putting in appearance. It's often included in local meals and is something of an acquired taste.

Dog: While foreign perceptions tend to suggest that Asia is far more into dog meat than it actually is, the majority of Vietnam's canine consumption occurs in the north, where dog is still considered something of a delicacy. Down south, you're less likely to find locals indulging in dog, but there are still people who enjoy it every now and again, and Saigon does have a small street dedicated to the sale of canine meat. Most meals are prepared in much the same way as chicken, beef, or other meats—roasted, steamed, boiled, or barbecued—and served with rice or added into a soup.

With a government ban on the sale of dog meat and growing concerns over its safety, this delicacy may be harder to come by over the next few years. The harsh reality of this dish is that most of the animals slaughtered and prepared are actually pets or strays that have been kidnapped. Given the persistence of rabies in Vietnam, contaminated meat is a risk. Many people also believe that canine meat is at its best when the animal has suffered, so the dogs are often killed in a brutal way. As demand increases throughout Southeast Asia, more and more dogs are being smuggled into Vietnam and killed, and the quality, safety, and humane treatment of these animals is fast decreasing.

Embryonic duck egg: Known locally as *hot vit lon* and more widely as *balut*, embryonic duck eggs are regularly consumed in Vietnam and several Southeast Asian countries, namely the Philippines. Larger and more dense than your average chicken egg, *hot vit lon* is consumed when the fetus is 19-21 days old—still too small to hatch but old enough that its wings, feet, beak, and eyes are visible. Like any egg, the yolk is thick and a little dry, while the tiny bird makes up the majority of the shell. *Hot vit lon* is commonly enjoyed on the street with salt, pepper, or lime and an ice-cold beer.

Pigeon: In the mountainous north where protein is scarce, small birds are often a part of local fare. Creatures like pigeons and other forest-dwelling birds are grilled and eaten with rice and rice wine or beer.

Rice paddy rat: In the Mekong Delta and parts of Cambodia, rice paddy rats are a delicacy. Much cleaner than their city-dwelling counterparts, these countryside rodents are sold at the market on a seasonal basis and usually grilled, barbecued, or boiled. Dishes are best enjoyed with beer or rice wine.

Snake: Particularly in the north, snake meat is a delicacy. While some creatures are simply slaughtered and prepared like any other meal, eating snake is more often than not an almost ritualistic experience. First, the live animal is slit from neck to tail, slicing open the skin to reveal its flesh, before its blood and bile are drained into separate shot glasses and combined with rice wine. After the blood has been consumed, the snake's still-beating heart is removed and swallowed by the guest of honor.

of chicken and beef, though fish sometimes makes an appearance. Hot dishes like *chao* (rice porridge) and what is officially considered the country's best pho are native to the north, as is *bun cha,* a simple but mouthwatering combination of cold rice noodles, fish sauce, pickled vegetables, and grilled meat.

Things heat up in the central region, where spicier dishes like *bun bo Hue* (spicy beef noodle soup) are all the rage, not to mention the dozens of tiny, bite-sized foods found in the Nguyen dynasty's former capital, including *banh beo* (steamed rice cake with shrimp paste), *banh duc* (sticky steamed rice cake), *banh loc* (steamed shrimp and pork fat dumplings), and *banh hoi* (bundles of rice vermicelli).

By the time you reach Saigon and the rest of the south, foods are sweeter, with more sugar found in local dishes. Whether it be the massive river fish of the Delta or the tasty grilled octopus of the southern coast, seafood features heavily in southern cuisine and many dishes are fried, including all varieties of *banh xeo* (savory pancakes), as well as a handful of local specialties like *banh khot* (Vung Tau's delicious, bite-sized rice cakes).

BEER AND RICE WINE

Along with local favorites like southern Saigon Red or Huda, a brew from the central region, freshly made beers are a popular fixture during local happy hours. *Bia tuoi* (fresh beer) is a locally produced lager sold in 100-liter barrels to small shops across town (also called *bia hoi*), particularly in Hanoi. Often going for as little as VND4,000 a glass on the street, this watered-down beverage is incredibly popular up north and must be drunk the day it is made, as its shelf life is very short. Men regularly gather at *bia hoi* after close of business to enjoy a few drinks and catch up. While fresh beer would not under most circumstances be considered a fine beer, the cultural experience of hanging out at a *bia hoi* in the city is well worth the dirt-cheap price tag.

locally brewed beer

Drinking in Vietnam

Though it is largely reserved for men, drinking is a large part of Vietnamese culture. As one of the world's top beer-drinking nations, this country takes its alcohol consumption seriously, as evidenced by the dozens of drinking slogans that can be heard during a weekend drinking session or at happy hour. Phrases like *mot tram phan tram* (100 percent, or bottoms up) and *khong say khong ve* (you can't go home until you're drunk) spell out the Vietnamese attitude towards imbibing. Drinking is a social event and is often accompanied by *do nhau* (drinking food), such as snails, grilled meat, or other savory snacks. Beer is enjoyed with ice and shared among the group. If you go out drinking with a local crowd, be prepared to clink glasses a lot: *Mot, hai, ba, DZO!* (One, two, three, CHEERS!) is a phrase commonly repeated throughout the night.

Drinking in Vietnam can be an enjoyable experience but it can also be a dangerous one. Drinking and driving is a common practice in a country where road safety is already dismal at best. Exercise the same good judgment you would when going out at home: Never get on the back of a motorbike with someone who has been drinking or appears to be drunk, and always opt for an alternative means of transportation in the event that someone in your party is not able to drive.

While it is not a widespread problem, methanol poisoning can occur as a result of poorly produced homemade alcohol or counterfeit spirits. This is a very serious condition that can result in permanent disability or life-threatening complications.

Much stronger than fresh beer, rice wine is a high-octane spirit that is often enjoyed in the countryside and becomes a major fixture during Tet, the Vietnamese lunar new year. Across Vietnam, locals make their own alcohol, storing it in massive plastic jugs for the coming festivities. Glutinous rice is steamed and left to sit for several days, adding yeast to the mixture, to produce a spirit that can carry a concentration of up to 22 percent alcohol. While you won't often find rice wine in local shops, it is everywhere in the countryside. In many cases, making local friends off the beaten path is likely to earn you at least a shot or two.

Conduct and Customs

GENERAL ETIQUETTE

Vietnam is a very polite country. Though Western-style customer service is not always observed in restaurants or hotels, you'll be hard-pressed to find people who are intentionally rude. Locals rarely raise their voices out of anger or show intense emotions in public. Daily interactions are handled calmly and politely. When problems arise, the typical Vietnamese reaction is often awkward laughter. This can be a frustrating and seemingly inappropriate response. In Vietnamese culture, showing anger is considered a lack of self-control and will likely cause the person you're dealing with to shut down, leaving you no better off than when you started.

As much as the average person is polite and respectful, the rules of etiquette, like most rules in Vietnam, are sometimes overlooked. Lining up, it seems, is the worst: people push, shove, and openly cut in front while waiting for a bus or at the supermarket checkout counter. If this happens, politely ask the person to move and you'll usually get a feigned surprise or even an apology, and most of the time that individual will get out of line. Acts like these are rarely meant to be rude; it's just that they were hoping you wouldn't say anything.

APPROPRIATE DRESS

Though you wouldn't know it in larger cities, Vietnam's sense of style tends to be rather conservative, with most people opting for long pants and shirts that cover their shoulders. Women in particular are usually more reserved, though sheer shirts are in fashion. In professional or religious settings, outfits that hit below the knee are appropriate for women and long pants are a must for men. At night all rules go out the window, as you'll see young Vietnamese women flying by on the back of a motorbike in sky-high stilettos and a mini skirt. For the most part, the same rules apply in Vietnam as in the United States: you wouldn't show up to work or to church in your party dress or shorts and flip-flops; if you visit a pagoda or an office building, the same holds true.

BODY LANGUAGE

Unlike Cambodia or Thailand, bowing in Vietnam, while still respectful, does not carry the same significance. Instead, when handing something to an elder or a stranger, for instance, it is polite to give the item with both hands as a sign of respect, or to offer the item with the right hand while placing the left hand on the right elbow. Certain gestures are inappropriate

Offering objects with two hands is considered a sign of respect.

here where they would not be at home. Crossing your forefinger and middle finger over one another, for instance, is a rude gesture in Vietnam. When beckoning someone, it's better to use an underhand motion.

Vietnamese culture dictates that the top of a person's head is the most sacred part of his or her body (because it is closest to God), while the soles of one's feet are the lowest. Touching the top of a person's head is considered impolite, particularly with children, as is showing a person the soles of your feet. In pagodas especially, directing the soles of your feet at the Buddha is considered an offensive gesture.

TABLE MANNERS

There are several Vietnamese dining habits that break with Western ideas of what is polite. Slurping your soup, talking with a full mouth, and shouting for the waiter are all acceptable practices at a local restaurant. You can shout *em oi!* to beckon a waiter over to your table. While it may seem odd at first, you'll want to get the hang of it, as servers don't check up on quiet tables and only bring the bill when you've asked for it. If you're visiting a street food stall or a more local restaurant, throwing rubbish like napkins and used toothpicks on the floor is also acceptable. This may seem unsanitary, but a restaurant employee will come by and sweep up any garbage that gets left on the floor. Occasionally, wastebaskets are positioned at the end of each table. If you're in doubt, take a look around: if you can see squeezed limes, napkins, and other rubbish strewn across the floor, then you're allowed to do the same.

When eating with a local family, Vietnamese hospitality dictates that no guest go hungry: in a Vietnamese house, you will eat until you're full and then some. Be warned that any time you empty your bowl it will be filled again before you have the chance to decline. Dining family-style means that anyone can pick at the assortment of meats and veggies on offer and drop some into your bowl, and people often do when guests are around. In situations like these, rice is served in a small *chen* (bowl) for each person, while the main dishes are set out in the middle. When eating, it is acceptable to pick up your *chen* and bring it closer to your mouth; as you reach the bottom of the bowl, you may lift it to your mouth and use your chopsticks to shovel the rice in. Take what is closest to you, as any piece you touch is yours, and always put the food in your *chen* first before bringing it to your mouth.

There are a long list of dos and don'ts regarding chopstick etiquette. For most transgressions, foreigners will likely be forgiven. Always lay your chopsticks parallel to one another, never crossed, and do not point them at other people, as these gestures are considered rude. It is also inappropriate to leave your utensils in the shape of a "V," and chopsticks should never be stuck upright into a bowl of rice, as this resembles incense sticks and is viewed as an omen of death.

LANGUAGE AND COMMUNICATION

As a nation still getting the hang of the tourism industry, Vietnam lacks an adequate number of fluent English speakers. In part due to the complexities of their own language, the Vietnamese have a great deal of trouble with English (and, it's safe to say, English-speakers face the same challenges with Vietnamese). Staying patient and simplifying your requests will go a long way to helping make yourself understood. In English, we often make requests more polite by adding extra words. For instance, at home you might say, "I was wondering if you could tell me where the restroom is?" For a weaker English speaker these extra words add confusion. Instead, "Excuse me, where is the toilet?" will make you more easily understood and locals will not take offense to the shorter sentences.

Whenever you arrange a service—whether it be a motorbike rental, a *xe om* ride, a day tour, or a cooking course—always be clear on the cost and the expectations of both parties before setting out, as this will help to prevent disagreements. Patience goes a long way. Expressing anger or being short with someone will keep you from gaining that person's respect.

WHAT TO PACK

Thanks to a steady influx of foreign visitors, Vietnam offers plenty of Western amenities, but some items are still hard to come by. Sunscreen, for instance, is almost never used among the local population and so can be difficult to track down in Vietnam. When you do find it, sunblock is overpriced and the locally produced version is not particularly effective. You're better off bringing your own sunscreen from abroad. The same goes for insect repellent. For women, feminine products are available at most pharmacies and drugstores, but tampons are less common, so bring your own.

Given the humidity, lightweight, breathable clothing and sturdy shoes are a wise choice for any traveler. Anyone planning to go pagoda-hopping should opt for at least one long-sleeved shirt and pants or shorts that reach the knee. A hat is a good idea as certain destinations like the Mekong Delta and Nha Trang are notably devoid of shade. While backpacking through Vietnam is a dirty business and your standard shorts-and-T-shirt attire is perfectly acceptable, pack one or two nice outfits if you plan to hit the town in the bigger cities like Hanoi or Saigon. You will likely need a raincoat at one time or another while in Vietnam, but bringing your own is optional, as cheap, plastic cover-ups are widely available.

OPPORTUNITIES FOR STUDY AND EMPLOYMENT

As job opportunities at home dwindle, more and more Western travelers are choosing to make a home in Asia, if only for a year or two. A combination of increasing tourism and growing demand for English-language education in Vietnam have created ample opportunities for foreigners looking to experience another part of the world and earn money at the same time. Short-term employment can be found at hostels and guesthouses around the country, where simple housework or other odd jobs are sometimes traded for room and board. For more permanent employment, most companies require you to make connections once you've already arrived in Vietnam. Websites like **VietnamWorks** (www.vietnamworks.com) provide insight into what's available from abroad.

If you plan to be in Asia for six months or more, ESL teaching is an excellent option. Jobs teaching English in Vietnam are widely available in Saigon and Hanoi, while employment in smaller cities like Danang is growing. Most English-teaching contracts range between six months and one year, and several schools within Vietnam offer ESL teaching certification courses, like the CELTA or TESOL, both of which are recognized internationally. **Apollo English** (www.apollo.edu.vn), **ILA** (www.ilavietnam.com), and **VUS** (www.vus.edu.vn) are reputable English teaching centers that employ foreign instructors. You can work under-the-table gigs with a tax-free hourly wage, but these businesses are far less reliable. In order to get a legitimate job with a reasonable salary, you'll need a Bachelor's degree in any field, a TESOL or CELTA certificate, a police background check from your home country or state, and a medical check to confirm that you are in good health. If you decide to teach in Vietnam, it is infinitely easier to apply for a work permit and a legitimate visa if you have an original copy of your Bachelor's degree notarized at home and your police check completed before you arrive rather than coordinating these documents from Vietnam, as the red tape can be exhausting.

Beyond teaching English, a variety of other opportunities are available but often require you to make connections within Vietnam first, which is why a teaching job is often the way foreigners get started in Vietnam. Once you've met some of your fellow expats and gotten to know the lay of the land, you can find jobs in anything from marketing and sales to graphic design, business, science, and even the food and beverage industry.

ACCESS FOR TRAVELERS WITH DISABILITIES

Vietnam is not easily accessible for travelers with physical disabilities, particularly anyone who uses a wheelchair. Elevators are seldom available outside of major cities, streets and sidewalks are often crumbled and aging, and many of Vietnam's tourist attractions require some mobility. Major cities are better equipped to accommodate travelers with disabilities, including Ho Chi Minh City, Danang, and Hanoi. Particularly around Danang and Hoi An, a popular area for many older travelers, businesses and accommodations will likely be more equipped to serve tourists with disabilities.

WOMEN TRAVELING ALONE

Vietnam is safe for female tourists. Women are able to travel freely without much harassment. Solo women will receive their fair share of lighthearted marriage proposals and occasional pestering from local men, but this rarely results in any serious issues. Always be polite but firm when encountering unwanted attention and, once you have made your point, ignore the other party. This is more effective than continuing to respond.

GAY AND LESBIAN TRAVELERS

Gay and lesbian travelers will find that Vietnam is an accepting place. The speed with which Vietnam has come to accept its own LGBTQ community is incredibly heartening. In little more than a few years, large swaths of the urban population have come to understand, albeit tentatively, the presence of homosexuality in local society. In 2015, the Vietnamese government legalized same-sex weddings, with one high-ranking official even publicly supporting same-sex marriage. (Note the difference here between a wedding and a marriage.) Since 2012, Hanoi has held an annual **VietPride festival** (www.vietpride.info) and continues to push for greater recognition of LGBTQ Vietnamese throughout the country. For the most part, many locals are happy to live and let live, though public displays of affection from any couple—gay or straight—are usually discouraged. More and more young Vietnamese are empowered to come out and a handful of great organizations in the major cities are improving social perceptions of LGBTQ people in Vietnam. The countryside is still a conservative place where tolerance may be less forthcoming.

Health and Safety

VACCINATIONS

As per **CDC** (Centers for Disease Control and Prevention, www.cdc.gov/travel) guidelines, all travelers to Vietnam should be up-to-date on routine vaccinations before going abroad. It is recommended that travelers receive vaccinations against Hepatitis A and typhoid, both of which can be spread through contaminated food or water. For more adventurous travelers and anyone planning to visit remote areas in Vietnam or to stay for a long time, vaccinations against Hepatitis B and Japanese encephalitis are encouraged, as well as preemptive rabies prophylaxis.

Malaria

Though malaria is less common in Vietnam than other parts of Southeast Asia, this flu-like, potentially fatal illness still exists in the southern half of the country. CDC guidelines recommend that travelers to rural areas in the south take malaria prophylaxis. Check with your doctor to find out which prophylaxis is best for you, as Vietnam's particular strain of malaria is resistant to certain drugs. There are many side effects associated with malaria prophylaxis, including minor annoyances like upset stomach, nausea, and sensitivity to sunlight but also more serious issues such as anxiety, hallucinations, and even seizures. Many travelers forgo using malaria drugs and instead take extra precautions in covering up and preventing mosquito bites. While DEET repellents are not intended for long-term use, a couple days of strong insect repellent should be fine. If you believe that you have contracted malaria, seek medical attention immediately. When caught early, malaria is very treatable.

Rabies

For anyone traveling to remote areas, spending a lot of time outdoors, or planning to travel by bicycle, the rabies vaccination is recommended, as people continue to die from the disease in Vietnam each year. Almost always fatal, rabies can be transmitted to humans through a bite or scratch from monkeys, cats, dogs, and bats. Avoid touching animals in Vietnam, even pets, as they are often left to their own devices and not cared for in the same way as Western pets. If you are bitten or scratched by a wild animal, wash the wound immediately with soap and water before seeking medical attention. Typically, an unvaccinated person requires a series of five shots following rabies exposure; those who have had preemptive prophylaxis need only two shots as soon as possible following the encounter. Due to the number of wild animals in Vietnam, rabies vaccines are widely available in the country and can be administered almost anywhere, including remote areas.

HEALTH

Allergies

Travelers with severe allergies may have trouble in Vietnam, especially those allergic to shellfish and peanuts, as these are frequent ingredients in Vietnamese cuisine. Cross-contamination is difficult to manage at street carts or in local restaurants, and even if you explain your dilemma to a local server there is no guarantee that the message will be understood. Take care to read all packaged foods and bring your own means of treatment, such as an EpiPen, to counter an allergic reaction. In the event of a severe allergic reaction, seek medical attention immediately.

Traveler's Diarrhea

One of the less glamorous facets of traveling, traveler's diarrhea is common among visitors to Vietnam, particularly those who enjoy street food. Some guidelines urge visitors to avoid roadside food carts as well as ice and fresh vegetables, but this may make your stay more expensive, not to mention detract from the overall experience. Avoiding specific street vendors or restaurants whose kitchens appear unclean or have food that has been sitting out for some time will help to decrease your risk of traveler's diarrhea and other food-borne illnesses. Dishes that are served hot and meat and veggies that have been fried, grilled, or otherwise prepared with high heat should be fine. In many cases, a good street food restaurant will prepare their meals in plain sight, giving you the ability to see the kitchen for yourself. When it comes to dishes like pho, *bun bo* (spicy beef noodle soup), and *banh xeo* (savory Vietnamese pancakes), fresh greens are usually served on the side, so you are able to easily avoid them if you so choose.

Regarding beverages, the ice at most restaurants in backpacker areas and higher-end eateries is safe to consume. Tap water is not meant for anything beyond showers and brushing your teeth. Though water can be boiled, nearly everyone in the country drinks bottled water or *tra da,* a light tea served at local restaurants.

In the event that you find yourself with traveler's diarrhea, it's best to stick to bland foods and proper restaurants for a day or two until your symptoms subside. Over-the-counter anti-diarrheal drugs like Imodium are available both in Vietnam and at home. If the issue persists, visit a doctor, who will prescribe something stronger. If you visit a physician in the United States prior to your trip abroad, ask about anti-diarrheal medicines, as procuring medications at home is generally safer than doing so in Vietnam.

Dengue

One of the few more serious illnesses that exists in Vietnam's cities as well as in rural areas is dengue. Passed through mosquito bites, the disease causes fever, headaches, and muscle and joint pain along with flu-like symptoms. There is no vaccination for dengue. Anyone who believes to be suffering from the disease should seek medical attention, as dengue is highly treatable but can become fatal if left unchecked. Should you become ill, avoid mosquitoes, rest, stay hydrated, and, of course, see a doctor. Acetaminophen-based pain killers can be used to relieve muscle and joint aches, but you should avoid any medications with aspirin, ibuprofen, or naproxen. Take extra care to monitor your health as the symptoms recede; in rare cases, dengue can turn into a fatal condition just as the initial symptoms appear to subside. If you experience difficulty breathing, pale or clammy skin, persistent vomiting, bleeding from your nose or gums, or red spots on your skin, go to a hospital immediately, as these may be signs of a more serious condition.

Zika Virus

In April 2016, Vietnam's Ministry of Health confirmed the country's first Zika cases. Since then, the southern half of Vietnam has seen a marked increase in the spread of the illness, with dozens of reported cases in Ho Chi Minh City alone. Popular tourist destinations like Nha Trang and the Mekong Delta region have also been affected. A handful of international travelers have returned home after a trip to Vietnam and begun showing symptoms of the virus. Vietnam has also reported one case of Zika-linked microcephaly in the Central Highlands.

The virus is currently considered endemic in Vietnam, meaning occasional cases may follow. It's unlikely that the rate of Zika infection will be so high as to cause an epidemic. As of the time of writing, Vietnam had recorded Zika cases in Saigon, Binh Duong, Nha Trang, and Phu Yen; it's expected the virus will also spread to northern Vietnam.

While there is no vaccination to prevent Zika infection, travelers can limit their risk by wearing long sleeves and mosquito repellent during the day and opting for air-conditioned accommodations at night. Check the CDC website (www.cdc.gov) for the most up-to-date information.

Methanol Poisoning

Though this is still a rare problem among travelers, a handful of cases in recent years have raised the need for awareness regarding methanol poisoning. More commonly known as wood alcohol, methanol is the cousin of ethanol, the type of alcohol found in spirits like vodka, whiskey, or rum. Where ethanol can leave you with a bad headache, a queasy stomach, and all the other trappings of a regular hangover, methanol is much worse, with even small doses causing serious side effects or even death.

As a means of cutting costs, some local businesses attempt to create their own homemade versions of alcoholic spirits using this substance, which they then sell to local bars, some of whom don't even know they're purchasing counterfeit booze. Regardless, unsafe amounts of methanol, which can be virtually undetectable in a mixed drink, have found their way into the hands of locals and travelers. Symptoms of methanol poisoning may not show up until as late as 72 hours after initial exposure and can often mirror the predictable symptoms of intoxication or a hangover, including confusion, dizziness, headaches, nausea, vomiting, and inability to coordinate muscle movements. In more serious cases, it can cause loss of vision; kidney, heart, and respiratory failure; gastrointestinal bleeding; and seizures, the combination of which can prove fatal.

It is extremely important to exercise caution when going out on the town, particularly in backpacker areas and in certain cities like Saigon and Nha Trang. Cheap drinks are available everywhere, but if a price seems too good to be true then it probably is. Purchasing your own spirits from a supermarket or chain convenience store is safer than opting for the local corner store. At the bar, if you order a drink and something doesn't seem right—the taste is particularly sweet or harsh, or the beverage is discolored—don't bother finishing it. For the most part, higher-end bars and lounges are safer than local watering holes or cheap backpacker spots. If all else fails, stick to beer and wine. Should you or a friend become a victim of methanol poisoning, go to a hospital immediately.

Insects

The local mosquito population continues to pester everyone in Vietnam. When traveling both in the city and throughout the countryside, take care to cover up at dawn and dusk, when insects are out in the greatest numbers, and use insect repellent. While it is possible to find repellent sprays in Vietnam, it's better to purchase them at home or in neighboring countries like Thailand, as these products can be more difficult to come by in-country and are usually more expensive. Avoid leaving your hotel room windows open at night and, if possible, sleep with the air-conditioning on or use a mosquito net around your bed. While rare, bed bugs are also an occasional problem in Vietnam, particularly if you are staying in dormitory-style accommodations. Check thoroughly for the critters before climbing into bed.

Wild Animals

Vietnam's largest animal problems tend to stem from dogs and cats, many of which are technically pets but whose owners let them roam freely outside. In more remote areas, locals keep dogs for protection. Cyclists in particular will want to steer clear of these animals, as they've been known to chase bikes. Avoid touching animals, even if they appear to be pets. If you come into contact with an animal, wash your hands thoroughly.

Medical Services

Medical services in Vietnamese hospitals are dismal at best, with major overcrowding and sanitation problems. In larger cities, international facilities provide a reasonable level of quality and will usually suffice in the event of illness or minor emergencies. More serious cases may require airlifting to Singapore or Bangkok; all of this should be covered by adequate travel insurance.

Insurance

Travel insurance is a must for visitors to Vietnam, as even a healthy tourist can become the victim of an accident, and while local hospitals may be significantly cheaper than their American counterparts, the cost of quality medical care can add up. Check with your current insurance provider to see if you are covered outside of your home country and what exactly falls within your plan. Travel insurance can be purchased through providers such as **Travel Guard** (www.travelguard.com). For most minor illnesses and injuries, healthcare in Vietnam is inexpensive enough that you may be able to cover the costs on your own, but at the very least be sure that your insurance plan covers major accidents and injuries. Confirm your plan's payment policy, as some hospitals in Vietnam require cash up front in order to perform medical services, and emergency evacuations can run in the hundreds of thousands of dollars. For those keen on hiring a motorbike, most travel insurance does not cover road accidents if the driver is unlicensed.

CRIME

The vast majority of crime in Vietnam involves bending the rules in business. While violent crimes occur, these incidents rarely involve foreigners.

The most common trouble you'll encounter is petty theft, which, while frustrating, seldom turns dangerous or violent. The second greatest concern for foreign visitors is drugs, which are illegal in Vietnam: Possession in large amounts can garner the death penalty or a protracted sentence for offenders.

Pickpocketing and Petty Theft

Though it's a minor offense compared to more violent crimes, petty theft is a big problem in Vietnam, especially in urban areas. Foreigners just getting the hang of a new country are often the victims. Particularly at night and around backpacker areas, tourists stand out as easy targets. Bag snatching, pickpocketing, and burglary are frequent occurrences, even in broad daylight.

There are steps you can take to minimize vulnerability. When walking around town, opt for pockets that close and keep your belongings in sight at all times. When paying for purchases, avoid showing large amounts of money, as this makes you a target. Anyone carrying a backpack should wear both straps; shoulder bags are best worn across the body and on the side furthest from the street. Avoid walking near the sidewalk's edge, as thieves on motorbikes have been known to snatch purses, phones, and wallets, sometimes dragging the person along with them. The same rules apply when you're on a motorbike: place your bag or backpack in front of you, hugging it to your chest, and tuck any necklaces into your shirt, as they can be snatched, too. Whether you're on foot or on a motorbike, use caution when taking out your belongings in public; even if you're just answering a text message or finding directions on your cell phone, duck into a local shop and out of view. These tips may sound extreme, but the number of tourists who have been robbed multiple times on a single trip suggests that, while slightly over-the-top, such practices are necessary. At night, common sense should be exercised. Male or female, don't walk alone around town, avoid alleyways, and always take taxis rather than *xe om* after dark.

If you are robbed, especially at night, it's best to let the situation go. The majority of these criminals are after your monetary goods, not your life. Your first priority should always be your own safety; remember that goods are replaceable, your life is not.

Not everyone is out to steal your money. Locals are incredibly kind, and if you follow precautions, you are less likely to encounter trouble.

Drugs

Recreational drugs like marijuana, heroin, and synthetic tablets are both widely available and illegal in Vietnam. There is a harsh, zero-tolerance policy for drug trafficking and possession.

Information and Services

MONEY

Currency

The official currency of Vietnam is known as the dong. Bills come in denominations of VND500, VND1,000, VND2,000, VND5,000, VND10,000, VND20,000, VND50,000, VND100,000, VND200,000, and VND500,000. Refuse ripped or torn bills, particularly those with denominations of VND10,000 or higher, as they are often rejected by shops and local businesses and you may find yourself stuck with money you cannot spend.

Exchange Rates

At the time of writing, the exchange rate for the Vietnam dong is roughly VND22,000 to one U.S. dollar. Current rates can be found online at **Oanda** (www.oanda.com) and **XE** (www.xe.com). Businesses within Vietnam operate on a rate that fluctuates between VND20,000 and VND23,000.

Changing Money

Most major tourist destinations have proper currency exchange kiosks, in addition to the countless hotels, restaurants, travel agencies, and gold shops that offer exchange services at various rates. While exchange kiosks are usually not affiliated with a bank, they are safe to use, as counterfeit currency is not a major problem in Vietnam. Ripped or torn bills are not accepted by many local businesses. If you receive any bills in this state, or if they are noticeably worn or faded, ask to have them switched out.

ATMs

ATMs are everywhere in Vietnam, with even the most remote destinations having at least one or two machines. Major cities often have ATMs from international banks such as ANZ, HSBC, Citibank, and Commonwealth Bank, as well as domestic institutions like Sacombank, Techcombank, and Vietcombank. Most domestic ATMs charge minimal fees for using their machines. International institutions sometimes charge more, though the cost rarely exceeds VND10,000 per withdrawal.

Bank Hours

For international banks, business hours are 8am-5pm; domestic institutions follow the same schedule but sometimes close earlier, at 4pm or 4:30pm, and almost always break for lunch, closing at 11am or 11:30am and reopening at 1pm or 1:30pm. All banks are open Monday-Friday, with some open on Saturday mornings as well.

Traveler's Checks

While it is possible to cash traveler's checks in certain banks in major cities, these are often far more trouble than they're worth. Not every financial institution will cash them and, when they do, many banks include fees and surcharges that eat away at the actual value of the check. **Vietcombank** (tel. 04/3824-3524, www.vietcombank.com.vn) is one of the few institutions that accepts traveler's checks, though the service is only provided in larger cities and not nationwide. With the availability of ATMs all over the country and the lack of places in which a stolen bank card could be used, you're better off bringing plastic and withdrawing money from a machine.

Costs

Every price, from food and accommodations to shopping, is up for negotiation. In major cities, a good local meal can go for as little as VND15,000-20,000 at a street stall to as much as VND200,000 in a restaurant. In these instances, what you pay for is the atmosphere—more often than not, the food at a small hole-in-the-wall shop or street cart is just as good, if not better, than what you'll find at a high-end restaurant in the trendier part of town. When eating street-side it is a good idea to ask the price beforehand, as vendors occasionally try to rip off tourists by doubling or tripling the bill at the end. You can avoid being had by agreeing upon the cost from the beginning.

Other goods and services are trickier to gauge in terms of cost. Prices fluctuate depending upon location. More tourist-heavy areas like Phu Quoc or Hoi An are often more expensive, while less-visited areas like the Mekong Delta and the Central Highlands tend to be a fraction of the cost. With prices changing all the time, it's difficult to say what an appropriate amount is for any given good or service.

Bargaining

In markets and shops across the country, bargaining is a common practice. Prices for everything from fresh produce to clothing to motorbike rides are up for negotiation. It is often expected that you'll haggle for goods and services if a price tag is not affixed to them. While it can be difficult to discern what a fair price is, your best bet is to ask around, gauge the average asking price of a few vendors, and then cut that number by 20-40 percent. In some cases this will be too much, in other cases too little. Take care not to enter into negotiations with a vendor unless you actually want the product. It's perfectly acceptable to ask the price of an item out of curiosity, but once you begin haggling it's assumed that you actually intend to buy the item.

Tipping

Outside of high-end restaurants, tipping is not required, nor is it a common practice. Some businesses take on a service charge for their employees, but you are not obligated to include something extra unless you feel inclined to do so. The only exception is in spas and massage parlors where tips are usually expected and you may even be asked to fill out a gratuity form after your massage. In this case, VND40,000 and up is usually acceptable. If you decide to leave a gratuity elsewhere, the amount really is up to you: In a country where one U.S. dollar can buy a meal, a motorbike ride, or even a pair of shoes, any extra cash you leave will be appreciated.

MAPS AND TOURIST INFORMATION

Vietnam is not great at providing accurate or detailed plans of the national road system. Cheap walking maps can be found in many towns. For anyone on a serious navigational mission, the only decent Vietnamese atlas is called *Tap Ban Do Giao Thong Duong Bo Viet Nam* and runs about VND300,000 in local bookshops.

The efficacy of local tourism offices varies depending upon the location. Places like Hanoi and Hoi An are packed with tour companies and travel agents who are willing to help, while a place like Con Dao, one of Vietnam's most remote islands, has maybe one or two English-speaking businesses.

COMMUNICATIONS AND MEDIA
Postal Services

Postage in Vietnam is cheap, with postcards traveling halfway around the world for VND10,000-20,000. The same goes for mail, but once you ship larger packages abroad the costs skyrocket, and in many cases there is no guarantee that the item will arrive at all. Most mail arrives at its destination within 2-3 weeks.

Area Codes

The country code for Vietnam is +84. Each city or province has its own area code, which is included in all phone numbers listed in this book. When calling locally, phone numbers can be dialed as they are listed here. International calls require 1, followed by the country code, but without the zero that appears at the beginning of each number in this book.

Cell Phones

Cell phones in Vietnam run on a pay-as-you-go basis and can be purchased new or used in most cities. For travelers, dirt-cheap brands like Nokia are useful and cost-effective; SIM cards are usually sold with the cell phone.

Internet Access

With the exception of the most remote corners of the country, Internet access in Vietnam is widespread. You can easily find Wi-Fi in local cafés and restaurants, while a smaller number of Internet and gaming cafés with computers are also available. Most hotels in major cities keep a desktop computer in the lobby for guests to use.

Local Newspapers and Magazines

A handful of national publications come out daily, weekly, or monthly in English, namely *Tuoi Tre* (www.tuoitrenews.vn), the online English-language version of the Vietnamese paper of the same name, and **VnExpress** (www.e.vnexpress.net), an online newswire. **Saigoneer** (www.saigoneer.com) is a good source of news as well as information on local history, social issues, arts and culture, and food. **Hanoi Grapevine** (www.hanoigrapevine.com) provides up-to-date event listings for Hanoi, while Saigoneer does the same for HCMC.

Monthly magazines geared toward expats are available for free in the country's two main hubs, Hanoi and Saigon, namely *AsiaLIFE* (www.asialifemagazine.com), *The Word* (www.wordhanoi.com or www.wordhcmc.com), and *Oi* (www.oivietnam.com).

Local Television

Local television leaves much to be desired, especially because only a few channels play programs in English. Popular foreign channels like National Geographic and Animal Planet broadcast English-language programming, while Star World and AXN are filled with dated prime time American sitcoms and reruns of *CSI*. All of these channels can be found on basic cable, along with at least one English-language news station. Hotels and restaurants with specific television packages carry European sports channels, the international version of ESPN, sometimes HBO, Star Movies, a regional channel featuring Western films, and Cinemax.

WEIGHTS AND MEASURES

Vietnam uses the metric system. Temperatures are recorded in Celsius, distances in kilometers, and weight in kilograms.

Resources

Glossary

ao dai: traditional Vietnamese garment

banh bao: steamed pork dumpling

banh beo: steamed rice flour cake

banh mi: Vietnamese bread, or a sandwich made out of this bread

banh trung thu: moon cake, a round, dense pastry whose reputation is not unlike fruitcake at Christmas—pretty, ornamental, and not nearly as delicious as it looks

banh xeo: savory Vietnamese pancakes

bia hoi: locally brewed beer (a variant is called *bia tuoi*); also the name for the shops that sell this beer

bun bo Hue: soup with beef and rice noodles, a specialty of Hue

bun cha: grilled meat and rice noodles in fish sauce, a Hanoian specialty

bun nem vit: soup with rice noodles, fresh greens, and duck spring rolls

bun thit nuong: rice noodles and grilled pork

cai luong: a popular form of traditional Vietnamese music

ca phe sua da: iced coffee with milk

ca phe trung: egg coffee

ca tru: ancient chamber music

cha ca: pan-fried fish

chao: rice porridge

com chay: vegetarian food

com cháy: a Ninh Binh specialty made from rice that is sun-dried, then fried

com ga: Hoi An-style chicken and rice

dan nhi: a musical instrument, resembling a two-stringed violin

doi moi: series of economic reforms instituted in the mid-1980s that transitioned Vietnam to a market economy

do nhau: drinking food

giay: paper

hu tieu: a southern-style rice noodle soup

khach san: hotel

linga-yoni **statue:** a statue representing male and female energies

mam tom: fermented shrimp paste

mua roi: water puppet

nem cua be: square-shaped seafood spring rolls

nha hang: restaurant

nha nghi: guesthouse

nha thuoc tay: pharmacies
nha tro: very basic hotel, a step down from a guesthouse, *nha nghi*
nuoc cham: a diluted fish sauce
phap lam: handicraft of enamel on metal, native to Hue
quat: paper fan
roi nuoc: water puppet theater
tap hoa: convenience store
xe om: motorbike taxi
xoi: sticky rice; popular street food
yen sao: edible bird's nests sold as souvenirs in Nha Trang

Vietnamese Phrasebook

The Vietnamese language consists of six tones. The rising, falling, flat, low, broken, and question tones can morph a single group of letters into any number of different words. Take *ma,* for instance, which can mean ghost (*ma*), horse (*mã*), grave (*mả*), mother (*má*), rice seedling (*mạ*), or which (*mà*), depending upon the tone. It is for this reason that most newcomers to the language have difficulty. Even the slightest change in tone can render a word contextually incomprehensible.

To make matters more challenging, most consonant sounds in Vietnamese are enunciated farther back in the speaker's mouth. When you make the "d" sound in English, for example, your tongue strikes the top of your mouth behind the teeth. In Vietnamese, the same letter is pronounced by striking near the center of the roof of your mouth, producing a duller version of the "d" sound, as in *đi* (to go) or *đỏ* (red). Add to that extra vowel sounds like *ơ* (pronounced "uh") and *ư* (pronounced like the "ou" in could) and you've got your work cut out for you.

On paper, Vietnamese is an easier language. Verbs require no conjugation and can be used without the past or future tense. Pronouns are not always necessary. In informal conversation, sentences can be shortened to nothing more than a few words and still retain their meaning. Vietnamese is also one of the only languages in the region to use a Roman alphabet, which makes navigating most cities and towns infinitely simpler, even for someone who doesn't speak the language.

PRONUNCIATION
A handful of letters are pronounced differently in Vietnamese than in English.

Vowels
a   like ah, as in "ant"
ă   like uh, as in "cut"
â   like uh, as in "an"
e   like eh, as in "echo"
ê   like ay, as in "say"

i like ee, as in "see"

o like aw, as in "cot"

ô like oh, as in "broke"

ơ like uh, as in "fun"

u like oo, as in "food"

ư like ouh, as in "could"

y like ee, as in "bee"

Consonants

c a muted "c" sound, like a half-step between "c" and "g"

d like y, as in "you"

đ like d, as in "dog"

gi like y, as in "you"

nh like ny, as in "canyon"

ph like f, as in "phone"

qu like kw, as in "question" (northern) or like w, as in "wood"

x like s, as in "sink"

BASIC EXPRESSIONS

Hello./Goodbye. *Xin chào.*

How are you? *(Bạn) có khỏe không?*

I'm fine, thanks. And you? *Tôi khỏe. Còn bạn?*

Thank you. *Cảm ơn.*

You're welcome./No problem. *Không có gì./Không sao.*

yes *có*

no *không*

I don't know. *Tôi không biết.*

Please wait a minute. *Xin (bạn) chờ một phút.*

Excuse me./I'm sorry. *Xin lỗi.*

Pleased to meet you. *Rất vui gặp bạn.*

What is your name? *(Bạn) tên gì?*

Do you speak English? *(Bạn) biết tiếng Anh không? or (Bạn) nói tiếng Anh được không?*

I don't speak Vietnamese. *Tôi không biết tiếng Việt. or Tôi không nói tiếng Việt được.*

I don't understand. *Tôi không hiểu.*

How do you say ... in Vietnamese? *... tiếng Việt là gì?*

My name is ... *Tôi tên là ...*

Would you like ...? *(Bạn) có muốn ... không?*

Let's go to ... *Chúng ta hãy đi ...*

TERMS OF ADDRESS

Vietnamese terms of address vary depending upon the relationship between the speaker and the person to whom he or she is speaking. There are dozens of pronouns to signify the gender and age of a person as well as the level of intimacy between two people. A mother and her child, for instance, would and a young student would use *cô* (female teacher) or *thầy* (male teacher) and *con* (in this context, student).

For most travelers, these terms won't be necessary. On the road, most of your interactions will only require you to use pronouns of age and gender. It's simplest to use the neutral pronoun *tôi* when referring to yourself.

When visiting a restaurant or shop, a waiter or shop assistant will likely refer to you as *anh* (slightly older male) or *chị* (slightly older female) and themselves as *em* (a younger person), not necessarily because you are older, but because it shows respect.

If you happen to choose the incorrect pronoun, the other party will politely set you straight before continuing the conversation. In most cases, locals will be appreciative of your efforts and willing to let an error or two slide. Note that appreciation in Vietnamese culture is not always communicated in a way you might expect. Upon hearing a foreigner speak Vietnamese, locals are often quick to laugh. This is borne more out of surprise than anything and is not meant to offend.

In the chart below, the English pronouns "he" and "she" are not listed. With the exception of *tôi* and *bạn,* each of the pronouns below can be modified into "he" or "she" by tacking on the word *ấy* at the end. This means that *anh* (you, male) becomes *anh ấy* (he) or *cô* (you, female) turns into *cô ấy* (she).

RESOURCES
VIETNAMESE PHRASEBOOK

I (neutral) *tôi*
person of equivalent age *bạn*
slightly older male *anh*
slightly older female *chị*
younger person, male or female *em*
female old enough to be your mother *cô*
male old enough to be your father *chú*
male slightly older than your father *bắc*
female old enough to be your grandmother *bà*
male old enough to be your grandfather *ông*
niece/nephew (self-referential; used when speaking to someone old enough to be your parent) *cháu*
child (self-referential; used when speaking to someone old enough to be your grandparent) *con*
we (listener not included) *chúng tôi*
we (listener included) *chúng ta*
you (plural) *các anh/chị/em/bạn*
they *họ*

TRANSPORTATION

Where is...? *... ở đâu?*
How far is it to ... ? *... cách đây mấy cây số?*
How far is it from ... to ... ? *Từ ... đến ... cách mấy cây số?*
Do you know the way to ... ? *(Bạn) có biết đường đi ... không?*

bus station *bến xe*

bus stop *trạm xe búyt*

Where is this bus going? *Xe búyt này đi đâu?*

taxi cab *xe taxi*

train station *ga xe lửa* (south), *ga tàu* (north)

boat *chiếc tàu*

airport *sân bay*

I'd like a ticket to … *Tôi muốn mua vé đi …*

one way *một chiều*

round-trip *khứ hồi*

reservation *đặt vé*

Stop here, please. *Xin (bạn) dừng lại ở đây.*

entrance *lối vào*

exit *lối ra*

ticket office *phòng vé*

near *gần*

far *xa*

Turn left. *queo trái* (south), *rẽ trái* (north)

Turn right. *queo phải* (south), *rẽ phải* (north)

right side *bên phải*

left side *bên trái*

Go straight. *đi thẳng*

in front of *trước*

beside *bên cạnh*

behind *sau*

corner *góc*

stoplight *đèn đỏ*

here *ở đây*

street *đường phố*

bridge *cây cầu*

address *địa chỉ*

north *bắc*

south *nam*

east *đồng*

west *tây*

ACCOMMODATIONS

hotel *khách sạn*

guesthouse *nhà nghỉ*

Is there a room available? *Ở đây có phòng không?*

May I see it? *Tôi có thể coi phòng được không?*

What is the rate? *Giá phòng là bao nhiêu?*

Is there something cheaper? *(Bạn) có phòng rẻ hơn không?*

single room *phòng đơn*

double room *phòng đôi*

double bed *giường đôi*

dormitory *phòng tập thể*
key *chìa khóa*
reception *tiếp tân*
hot water *nước nóng*
shower *phòng tắm*
towel *khăn*
soap *sa bông*
toilet paper *giấy vệ sinh*
blanket *mền*
air-conditioning *máy lạnh* (south), *máy điều hòa* (north)
fan *quạt máy*
mosquito Net *màng*
laundry *giặt ủi*

FOOD

I'm hungry. *(Tôi) đói bụng.*
I'm thirsty. *(Tôi) khát nước.*
menu *thức đơn*
to order *gọi*
glass *ly*
fork *nĩa*
knife *dao*
spoon *muỗng*
chopsticks *đôi đũa*
napkin *khăn giấy*
soft drink *nước ngọt*
coffee/hot coffee/iced coffee *cà phê / cà phê sữa nóng / cà phê sữa đá*
coffee with milk *cà phê sữa*
tea/hot tea/iced tea *trà / trà nóng / trà đá*
bottled water *chai nước suối*
beer *bia*
juice *nước ép*
smoothie *sinh tố*
sugar *đường*
breakfast *ăn sáng*
lunch *ăn trưa*
dinner *ăn tối*
check, please *tính tiền*
eggs *trứng*
fruit *trái cây*
pineapple *trái thơm*
mango *trái xoài*
watermelon *dừa hấu*
papaya *đu đủ*
coconut *trái dừa*
lime *chánh*

durian *sầu riêng*
jackfruit *trái mít*
fish *cá*
shrimp *tôm*
chicken *thịt gà*
beef *thịt bò*
pork *thịt heo* (south), *thịt lợn* (north)
tofu *đậu hủ*
fried *chiên* (south), *rán* (north)
grilled *nướng*
boiled *luộc*
spicy *cay*

SHOPPING

money *tiền*
bank *ngân hàng*
Do you accept credit cards? *Ở đây có nhận thẻ tín dụng không?*
How much does it cost? *Cái này là bao nhiêu tiền?*
expensive *mắc tiền* (south), *đắt tiền* (north)
too expensive *mắc qúa* (south), *đắt quá* (north)
cheap *rẻ*
more *nhiều hơn*
less *ít hơn*
a little *một ít*
too much *quá nhiều*

HEALTH

Help me, please. *Xin (bạn) giúp tôi đi.*
I am sick. *(Tôi) bị bệnh.*
Call a doctor. *Gọi cho bác sĩ đi.*
Please take me to ... *Xin (bạn) đưa tôi đến ...*
hospital *bệnh viện*
drugstore/pharmacy *nhà thuốc tây*
I'm allergic to ... *Tôi bị dị ứng với ...*
bees *con ong*
peanuts *đậu phọng*
seafood *hải sản*
I'm asthmatic. *Tôi bị suyễn.*
I'm diabetic. *Tôi bị bệnh đái đường.*
I'm epileptic. *Tôi bị động kinh.*
pain *đau*
fever *bệnh sốt*
headache *đau đầu*
stomachache *đau bụng*
burn *vết bỏng*
nausea *buồn nôn*

vomiting *bị mửa*
diarrhea *tiêu chảy*
antibiotics *thuốc kháng sinh*
aspirin *thuốc giảm đau*
penicillin *thuốc pênicilin*
pill, tablet *viên thuốc*
cream *kem*
contraceptive *cách ngừa thai*
condoms *bao cao su*
insect repellent *thuốc chống muỗi*
sunscreen *kem chống nắng*
sanitary pads *băng vệ sinh*
tampons *ống băng vệ sinh*
toothbrush *bàn chải đánh răng*
toothpaste *kem đánh răng*
dentist *nha sĩ*
toothache *nhức răng*

COMMON SIGNS

entrance *lối vào*
exit *lối ra*
men *đàn ông*
women *phụ nữ*
toilet *nhà vệ sinh / WC*
information *hướng dẫn / thông tin*
open *mở cửa*
closed *đóng cửa*
prohibited *cấm*

POST OFFICE AND COMMUNICATIONS

I would like to call… *(Tôi) muốn gọi cho…*
collect/collect call *thu thập gọi*
credit card *thẻ tín dụng*
post office *bưu điện*
airmail *thư gửi bằng máy bay*
letter *thư*
stamp *tem*
postcard *bưu thiếp*
registered/certified *thư bảo đảm*
box, package *hộp, gói*

AT THE BORDER

border *biên giới*
customs *hải quan*
immigration *nhập cư*
inspection *sự thanh tra*

passport *hộ chiếu*
profession *nghề nghiệp*
insurance *bảo hiểm*
driver's license *giấy phép lái xe, bằng lái*

AT THE GAS STATION

gas station *trạm xăng*
gasoline *xăng*
full *hết bình*
tire *bánh*
air *bơm xe*
water *nước*
oil change *thay dầu*
my … doesn't work *… của tôi bị hư*
battery *pin*
repair shop *tiệm sửa xe*

VERBS

to buy *mua*
to eat *ăn*
to climb *leo*
to make *làm*
to go, to leave *đi*
to walk *đi bộ*
to like *thích*
to love *yêu*
to work *làm việc*
to want *muốn*
to need *cần*
to read *đọc*
to write *viết*
to repair *sửa*
to stop *dừng lại*
to get off (the bus) *xuống xe*
to arrive, to come *đến*
to stay *ở lại*
to sleep *ngủ*
to look at *xem*
to look for *tìm*
to give *đưa*
to carry *mang*
to have *có*

NUMBERS

one *một*
two *hai*

three *ba*
four *bốn*
five *năm*
six *sáu*
seven *bảy*
eight *tám*
nine *chính*
10 *mười*
11 *mười một*
12 *mười hai*
13 *mười ba*
14 *mười bốn*
15 *mười lăm*
16 *mười sáu*
17 *mười bảy*
18 *mười tám*
19 *mười chính*
20 *hai mười*
30 *ba mười*
100 *một trăm*
101 *một trăm lẻ một*
200 *hai trăm*
1,000 *một ngàn* (south), *một nghìn* (north)
10,000 *mười ngàn* (south), *mười nghìn* (north)
100,000 *một trăm ngàn* (south), *một trăm nghìn* (north)
1,000,000 *một triệu*
one-half *nửa phần*

TIME

What time is it? *Bây giờ là mấy giờ rồi?*
It's one o'clock. *Bây giờ là một giờ.*
It's four in the afternoon. *Bây giờ là bốn giờ chiều.*
It's noon. *Bây giờ là mười hai giờ trưa.*
It's midnight. *Bây giờ là mười hai giờ khuya.*
morning *sáng*
afternoon *chiều*
evening *tối*
one minute *một phút*
one hour *một giờ, một tiếng*

DAYS AND MONTHS

Monday *thứ hai*
Tuesday *thứ ba*
Wednesday *thứ tư*
Thursday *thứ năm*
Friday *thứ sáu*

Saturday *thứ bảy*
Sunday *chủ nhật*
January *tháng giêng*
February *tháng hai*
March *tháng ba*
April *tháng tư*
May *tháng năm*
June *tháng sáu*
July *tháng bảy*
August *tháng tám*
September *tháng chính*
October *tháng mười*
November *tháng mười một*
December *tháng mười hai*
today *hôm nay*
yesterday *hôm qua*
tomorrow *ngày mai*
a day *một ngày*
a week *một tuần*
a month *một tháng*
after *sau đây*
before *trước đây*
rainy season *mùa mưa*
dry season *mùa khô*
spring *mùa xuân*
summer *mùa hè*
winter *mùa đông*
fall *mùa thu*

Suggested Reading

HISTORY

Bartimus, Tad, Ed. *War Torn: Stories of War from the Women Reporters Who Covered Vietnam*. New York: Random House, 2002. Written by a group of women ranging from veteran journalists to twenty-something novices, this collection of memoirs presents a different side of Vietnam through the eyes of some of the first female reporters to cover a conflict from the front lines.

Herr, Michael. *Dispatches*. New York: Vintage Books, 1977. Lauded as one of America's most famous firsthand accounts of the Vietnam War, *Dispatches* is the product of Michael Herr's years as a journalist covering the conflict for *Esquire* magazine. The author went on to co-write *Apocalypse Now* and *Full Metal Jacket*.

Karnow, Stanley. *Vietnam: A History*. New York: Viking Press, 1983. The best-selling masterpiece of Stanley Karnow, a veteran journalist and historian who covered the Vietnam War and its aftermath both at home and abroad.

Mangold, Tom. *The Tunnels of Cu Chi*. New York: Ballantine Books, 1985. The fascinating story of the citizens of Cu Chi and the intricate system of tunnels they dug by hand to protect their homes. This book is a must-read for anyone interested in war history, with firsthand accounts of the harsh and unforgiving conditions of life underground and the struggles of NLF rebel fighters, as well as the stories of the U.S. Army's "tunnel rats" – a group of men who descended into the pitch-black tunnels to combat the enemy.

BIOGRAPHY AND MEMOIR

Duiker, William J. *Ho Chi Minh: A Life*. New York: Hyperion, 2000. A comprehensive biography of Vietnam's greatest leader and one of the 20th century's most influential politicians.

Pham, Andrew X. *Catfish and Mandala*. New York: Picador, 1999. In his early 30s, uncertain of his future and curious about his past, Andrew Pham set out from Saigon on a bicycle, heading up the coast of a Vietnam newly opened to the outside world, encountering the country's people, its problems, and its unbreakable spirit.

Sachs, Dana. *The House on Dream Street: Memoir of an American Woman in Vietnam*. Chapel Hill, NC: Algonquin Books, 2000. The memoir of a woman in her late 20s bound for Vietnam just as the country is beginning to open up after years of war and poverty.

FICTION

O'Brien, Tim. *The Things They Carried*. New York: Mariner Books, 1990. A semi-autobiographical collection of short stories, Tim O'Brien's fictional masterpiece follows a platoon of American soldiers in the jungles of Vietnam as they fight their way through the war.

Greene, Graham. *The Quiet American*. London: Vintage Books, 1955. An ominous and controversial novel twice adapted to film, Graham Greene's opus is set in early 1950s Saigon, a time and place rife with political tension and deception. This is perhaps one of the most famous English-language novels to be set in Vietnam.

Butler, Robert Olen. *A Good Scent from a Strange Mountain*. New York: Grove Press, 2001. A Pulitzer Prize-winning collection of short stories that peers into the lives of Vietnamese immigrants living in the United States as they navigate the cultural differences and war wounds of a turbulent history between the two nations.

TRAVEL INFORMATION

Rusty Compass

www.rustycompass.com

This outstanding, well-researched independent travel guide covers a wide range of Vietnamese destinations, providing travelers with helpful tips and recommendations as well as dozens of photos and videos. Run by Aussie expat Mark Bowyer, who has been based in Vietnam since the early 1990s, Rusty Compass is a great resource when planning your trip.

Travelfish

www.travelfish.org

A handy resource for anyone traveling in Southeast Asia, Travelfish offers independent reviews, practical information, and sound advice on countries throughout the region. The site's Vietnam section covers both major tourist destinations and several less-visited towns.

Vietnam Tourism

http://vietnamtourism.vn

A joint effort between the Vietnamese government and a tourism advisory board made up of local businesses, this site features suggestions on what to see and where to go throughout Vietnam.

PRACTICALITIES

U.S. State Department

www.travel.state.gov

Providing up-to-date information on all things Vietnam, the State Department's website stays abreast of current situations within the country and also offers useful information on practicalities such as border crossings, visas, and health and safety tips.

Centers for Disease Control

www.cdc.gov

Before traveling to Vietnam, check the CDC website for more country-specific information on vaccinations, malaria prophylaxis and other preventive measures.

BLOGS

The Comical Hat

www.thecomicalhat.wordpress.com

The odd and unorthodox musings of a local expat.

From Swerve of Shore

www.aaronjoelsantos.wordpress.com

A beautiful and vivid collection of photographs by Aaron Joel Santos, a Hanoi-based fashion photographer and photojournalist.

Sticky Rice

www.stickyrice.typepad.com

A street food blog devoted to discovering hidden gems along the winding, narrow streets of Hanoi.

Index

Photo Credits

Also Available

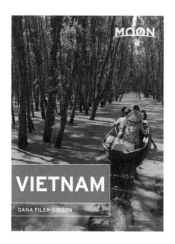

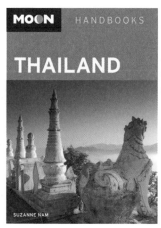

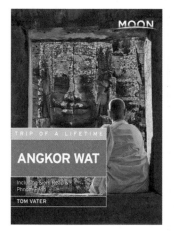

List of Maps